# Plundering Hell

## THE REINHARD BONNKE STORY

### By Ron Steele

D1324271

**marshalls**

Life Changing Books

Life Changing Books
Marshall Morgan & Scott
3 Beggarwood Lane, Basingstoke, Hants. RG23 7LP, UK

First published by Sceptre Publishers, P.O. Box 7461 Ravenmoor
1469, RSA.
First published in the UK by Marshall Morgan & Scott, 1984

Reprinted
Impression number
85  86  87  88  :  5  4  3  2

ISBN 0 551 01162 9

Printed and bound in Great Britain by
Anchor Brendon Ltd., Tiptree, Essex.

# CONTENTS

# CHAPTERS

**Publisher's Note**
R100 = 100 Rand
1 Rand is approx £1.64

# AUTHOR'S NOTE

THIS book was written to coincide with the opening and dedication of the world's biggest mobile tent. I have attempted to sketch a profile of the man behind one of the most ambitious mission projects ever attempted in Africa, if not the world. He sees not only the desperate physical plight of the continent, but the spiritual famine of millions of precious souls. This is the story of the man who has dared to accept the challenge to bring a life-changing experience to those who are trapped in an abyss of fear and spiritual desolation.

While not a definitive biography, I have attempted to flesh out something of the man who makes faith a living reality and who truly knows how to move mountains. I also hope that in some way I have portrayed his desire and zeal to exalt Jesus, the Person He loves more than his own life.

If Jesus were not alive today this story would have had no meaning and so I hope that readers will see Him as the central figure in this book. This book is dedicated to the Man who died for me — Jesus.

Ron Steele, Johannesburg 1984.

# FOREWORD

In the last five years the faith of two men has staggered me. In my presence I have heard them say what they felt God wanted them to achieve — and I ranked it as impossible. Those two men were Yonggi Cho and Reinhard Bonnke. Now I have lived to see the fulfilment of both of their faith dreams. In the case of Yonggi Cho he said that he was believing God for a church of 500,000 people by 1984 — he is now in sight of that preposterous target, and by the time you read this it will have been realised. In the case of Reinhard Bonnke he was talking about creating the world's biggest tent, capable of seating over 34,000 people. The technical difficulties alone were enough to deter any ordinary individual, let alone the financial costs. But listening to Reinhard Bonnke preach; fellowshipping with him and observing him at close quarters, I very soon realised that he was no ordinary man — but another of God's chosen vessels.

From his childhood he had the vision and call to Africa. It was a call to rank with that of God's summoning of the boy Samuel — and the response in Reinhard's young heart was just as whole-hearted as Samuel's. To meet this man is to realise immediately that he is utterly sold out to God — and Africa. Who but Almighty God would have dreamed of calling a blond German to become a successful evangelist to Africa? In the natural so many things seemed against it, but God never makes mistakes. Reinhard Bonnke has all the finest qualities that make the Germans such an out-standing race, but there is no arrogance with him, instead there is the humility that only Christ can create in a personality which has been fully surrendered to Him. Reinhard Bonnke has paid a price for his success; but his faith and commitment has not wavered. The result is a man who is stirring Africa in a way that it has never before been stirred. His burden is to take the Gospel of the Lord Jesus Christ (which he preaches with power and authority — and without compromise) from the Cape to Cairo. The Risen Lord constantly confirms His Word with signs following which are of New Testament calibre. Reinhard

Bonnke's story is a most amazing one — but I assure you, it is true. His audacity is a challenge to our feeble faith and lukewarm commitment; his faith is the kind you read about in Hebrews chapter 11. Here is another of God's heroes of faith. "Without faith it is impossible to please God." I have a feeling that this man's faith is most pleasing to God. And I have a feeling that his story as told in this book will challenge you to believe God for greater things in your own life. Bonnke is another living proof that "what you can conceive you can achieve". With God all things are possible.

Colin Whittaker
Editor, Redemption Tidings
and General Secretary
of the Assemblies of God.

# Plundering Hell

## THE REINHARD BONNKE STORY

**By Ron Steele**

"I will build My Church; and the gates of hell shall not prevail against it."

Matthew 16:18 (KJV)

All scripture quotations in this book are from the Kings James Version.

# CHAPTER ONE

## Escape

THEY came down the gangplank. A young man burdened with baggage, followed by his wife, hugging a young baby in her arms and trying not to lose her footing as the couple were jostled along by the disembarking passengers.

They stepped onto the dockside. The wind whipped across Durban Harbour as Reinhard and Anni Bonnke and their seven-month-old son, Freddy, stepped onto the continent of Africa. It was the end of May, 1967. As Reinhard stood there, slightly bewildered and feeling very far away from his church in northern Germany, he would never have dared to imagine what God had in store for him.

If he had, the 27-year-old Reinhard may well have turned around and shepherded his young family back aboard the ship and disappeared into the backwaters of northern Germany to live out the sedate life of a pastor.

He would never have dared to think that he would proclaim aloud in auditoriums around the world the almost boastful cry: "From Cape Town to Cairo, for Jesus!" But such things were in the future. For the moment the aspirant missionary to Africa was being showered with a typically warm South African welcome from pastors of the Apostolic Faith Mission, the denomination he has represented since setting foot on this continent. But of immediate concern to him was his young wife. Once the ship had passed through the Suez Canal the sea had become extremely rough and Anni, four months pregant, had been under constant medical care. For Anni Durban was heaven. It meant a good night's rest in a bed that didn't sway!

As the Bonnke's drove through the streets of Durban little did they realise that this was the beginning of a gospel saga that has become so daring and so revolutionary, that even as you read these pages the world is staggering at its concept.

For into the heart of this man God had placed a treasure and like a diamond, immense pressures and fiery heat would one day produce a glittering gem that would sparkle and captivate kings and princes, peasants and paupers.

Like the diamond this treasure was buried and hidden from view and it has taken years to dig it out, chisel and refine this precious gem of a man, who some have dared to call the Apostle to Africa.

He didn't come to southern Africa as a novice, though. He had tasted success as an evangelist in Germany. He had also been a successful pastor. But now his life was on the line as a missionary in one of the hostile continents of the world. A continent wracked with pain. A continent seething with revolution. A continent dying without hope. This was the challenge.

Would his boyhood dreams be fulfilled? That was the tantalising question mark that would furrow his brow in the months and years that lay ahead. There was no denying the supernatural signposts that God had planted along the pathway He had set before Reinhard.

The signposts in 1945, though, were ominous and Reinhard's young life was in desperate peril when the Bonnke family narrowly escaped being captured by the advancing Russian troops as the Germans retreated from the Eastern Front.

During World War Two Reinhard's father served in the Wehrmacht and the Bonnkes lived in Königsberg, capital of East Prussia.

It was a place of battered desolation in 1945 as streams of German troops and vehicles fell back in retreat as the Russian forces closed in on Königsberg. Russian planes flew over continually, bombing the retreating army and Reinhard, only five years old, vividly remembers the local post office building, which was just down the road from their house, receiving a direct hit.

His mother, a dedicated Christian, naively believed that she would be safe if she remained in her home. But, with the town ablaze, some German troops persuaded the family to flee.

It was the beginning of a nightmare journey, but also a miraculous one. It was night when Mrs Bonnke gathered the family together. Outside flames flashed skyward from bursting shells and burning buildings. With each one of her six children (five boys and a girl) carrying a bundle of personal belongings Mrs Bonnke led her precious brood out of their house and down to the main road.

It was a bewildering experience, but Reinhard does not recall being afraid. It all seemed like some exciting adventure. As the heaving, heavily laden army vehicles trundled past Mrs Bonnke waved her arms desperately to try and stop one of the trucks and so get a lift.

She refused to be separated from any of her children and the little group huddled together to comfort one another until at last a truck stopped and a voice yelled from the blackness of the cabin that there was room for only three. But Mrs Bonnke ignored the driver's restriction.

Reinhard remembers that night quite vividly: "Mother handed up my sister, then me and she just kept on pushing the children up until we were all crammed onto the truck and then she squeezed in as well."

It was a creaky, old wood-fired truck and as the gears grated they jerked off down the road. Reinhard remembers the brightness of flares being dropped by enemy planes, but he was so exhausted that he fell fast asleep in the arms of one of the soldiers in the truck.

It was still winter and when morning dawned everyone was cold, dirty and hungry. Nerves were raw as Russian fighters strafed the snaking line of trucks and bombs gouged ugly craters in the road.

The roadside was dotted with the grotesque sight of dead bodies. It was a terrifying journey and Reinhard stared wild-eyed as his young mind was assaulted by all this carnage. Night and day the smell of death was present.

When the trucks could take them no further Mrs Bonnke and the children took to the road. They trudged on foot for several days until they managed to get a lift again. Their escape route was across the Haff Sea. It was late winter and the ice was beginning to melt and the crossing was particularly treacherous with the vehicles often axle deep in the melting ice. Underneath surged the deep, freezing waters of the sea. The sovereign care of God is evident here because only days after their escape the Russians bombed the ice and thousands of refugees and soldiers lost their lives in the icy sea.

Eventually, bedraggled and weary, but still together, the family reached the port of Danzig (Gdansk today). The city was clogged with refugees and the only way of escape now was across the Baltic Sea.

In Danzig the family met an aunt and Mrs Bonnke's devout Christian mother. With thousands of other refugees they waited hopefully and prayerfully for a ship to carry them to Denmark and safety. They watched one ship, the Gustlov, crammed with 8 000 women and children, steam out of the harbour. Two days later they heard that the ship had struck a mine and only 200 people had survived.

Air raids increased and the Russians were drawing nearer when at last the Bonnkes were offered a berth on an ancient coal steamer.

Before the ship sailed his mother and grandmother read a portion from Isaiah which gave them all great comfort: "Thus saith the Lord which maketh a way in the sea and a path in the mighty waters."(Isaiah 43:16). The women were deeply moved and knelt in quiet prayer and committed themselves and the children to the Lord.

The morning that they went to board the ship the gangway was a seething mass of human bodies, pressing and shoving to get aboard. While boarding the air raid sirens shrieked out another warning and they wondered whether they would ever get aboard the ship. But eventually they were safely below deck and the ship steamed sluggishly out into the Baltic.

This was the start of another ordeal and another act

of God's Providence. The steamer ploughed through the waves and several times they were attacked from the air. One startling incident is still clearly etched on Reinhard's mind. He had just clambered up a rusty ladder to get to the toilet on top of the deck and as he peered out over the rails he watched in awe as a Russian plane, wreathed in flames, plumeted into the sea, a victim of the steamer's anti-aircraft guns.

Conditions on board were cramped. Everyone was herded together beneath the decks. There was no privacy. People were sick and the food was poor. Moans and groans filled the air. There were very few smiles and little to ease the tension of the refugees.

Suddenly, one afternoon, the ship shuddered and pitched violently and it seemed as if the steel plates would be ripped apart. They had struck a mine. The ship developed a heavy list and fear gripped the hopeless refugees who clung on to one another to steady themselves in the darkness and dampness below the decks.

Would the Bonnke's nightmare escape and their journey from Königsberg end in a watery grave? Mrs Bonnke held onto the Word of God she had read before leaving Danzig and comforted the children. Suddenly the ship began to right itself and the crew told the refugees that the pumps were coping with the flood of water that poured in below the decks.

Even today Reinhard admits that when he closes his eyes and casts his mind back to that time at sea he can hear those pumps clattering away, night and day. To all of those aboard those pumps sounded like a heavenly symphony as, miraculously, the ship stayed afloat. When recalling this incident to congregations around the world Reinhard quips, but with more than a degree of certainty, that "God never wanted my bones bleached at the bottom of the Baltic!"

The ship struggled on and a brave cheer of relief went up from the crew and the tear-stained refugees when the coast of Denmark came into sight. They were safe at last.

Looking back on that wartime escape . . . the dangers of air attack and the detonating of a mine the Lord had truly "made a a path" in the waters.

The Bonnkes were safe, but they had to wait 3 1/2 years before they were united with their father.

Reinhard's father had joined the army as a professional soldier in 1923 when he was 17. Like so many young people he was fired by the glory of German militarism. Reinhard's mother had become a Christian while still a young girl. His father's conversion to Christ had been quite dramatic. In fact, it had taken a miracle to convince him that Jesus Christ was alive and that God was real. He had contracted TB and was very ill when he was asked to go to a church revival meeting. Before going he had said that if God would heal him then he would believe that God was real. In a gracious act, and as part of a divine plan, the young professional soldier was healed, became a Christian and began to attend church. Later, he met and married the woman who played the organ in the local church.

As the final acts of the war were being played out Reinhard's father, who was an officer, was trapped with some other senior men at the port city of Danzig from where his wife and children had escaped earlier. There was a lone minesweeper in the harbour and a limited number of berths available. When his father told the others that he was married and had six children he got one of the remaining places and the ship left harbour. A few days later they were intercepted by a British naval vessel and the Germans were captured and put in a British PoW camp at Kiel. Meanwhile, Mrs Bonnke and her children lived as refugees in Denmark until at last they were returned to their war-ravaged homeland.

His father was eventually released and they were reunited as a family in the town of Glückstadt, late in 1948. Although he had not seen his father for almost four years, Reinhard instantly recognised him and ran into his outstretched arms. By this time his father was in the Lord's army and a fulltime pastor. The setting and preparation for Reinhard's spiritual development was now ready and God was about to move in a direct and personal way upon young Reinhard's life.

# CHAPTER TWO

## Preaching to the trees

In 1949, when Reinhard was nine-years-old he made Jesus his Saviour. His godly mother led him to the Lord, and then to make it "proper" little Reinhard had responded to an altar call in the local church so that all could see that he had given his heart to Jesus.

Even as a little boy, he was aware of spiritual things. Somehow he had grasped the words of Jesus: "Seek ye first the Kingdom of God . . ." He readily admits that he got up to the usual tricks and mischief that most young boys do but, mostly, he was a serious-minded child. The fact was that Jesus was the central person in his life. Sport held little thrill or attraction for him. Jesus was his boyhood hero — and still is. It would be true to say that when Reinhard gave his life to Jesus he fell in love with Him — totally. There was just never any place where any other love could ever get in. No wordly distraction could draw him away from the Saviour who had died for him. He did have an ear for music and learnt to play the piano and accordion and he shyly admits that one of his favourite "games" as a child was preaching to the trees in a nearby wood.

"A friend and myself would go off where nobody could see us or hear us and we would preach out our hearts to the trees. I must confess that my friend was always much better at preaching than I was and I wondered whether I would ever become good enough to stand behind a pulpit," admits Reinhard. Well, it turned out that his childhood friend never made the pulpit, in fact, never preached a sermon. Yet, the once shy and diffident boy preacher has turned the tall pines of the forest into the flesh and blood of the massive audiences that come to listen to one of this decade's most extraordinary evangelists. The thin alto voice that used to challenge the trees of northern Germany to repentance has shouted a million "hallelujahs" in a now familiar rasping baritone in churches, from Birmingham to Rio and from Toronto to Auckland. In small, pokey, dimly-lit halls, to glittering chrome and glass auditoriums, in tents and across the naked bush of Africa, Reinhard's voice has sounded the Good News.

His spiritual devotion was even misinterpreted by his parents who lived a frugal, pastoral life, governed by strict German discipline, and of course, the restraints of the holiness teaching of the Pentecostal church to which they belonged. And although little Reinhard was expected to attend church, prayer meetings were not obligatory.

Recalling those early days Reinhard says: "I was not allowed to go to mid-week prayer meetings, but I really wanted to go. I wanted to be there and when my mother saw me weeping because I couldn't go to a prayer meeting she relented. It was the first time she had every heard of a little boy crying because he couldn't go to a church meeting!"

It was at one of these mid-week meetings that a shaft of Divine light was shed on Reinhard's future life. It was the first of many dramatic supernatural encounters that were to punctuate the adventurous path that would lead him to one day challenge satan head-on, on the wind-swept veld of southern Africa.

During the little cottage meeting one of the women revealed that God had given her a vision and in it she saw a little boy breaking bread before thousands of Black people. Then she turned to Reinhard, who stood next to his father, and announced to everybody: "This is the little boy I saw in the vision." He was ten years old at the time.

Besides devouring his Bible Reinhard read the stories of famous missionaries and soon he was fired with the urge to go to the mission field. He heard visiting missionaries speak at his father's church and soon his mind was made up: he was going to be a missionary and not only that he was going to Africa. To his parents these were just the fond dreams of a young 11-year-old boy, but he refused to be put off. Some of his friends at church used to tease him, calling him the "little missionary", but inside Reinhard nursed and cherished the divine idea.

Then as a teenager Reinhard had a strange dream — again heaven's veil was parted and a small glimpse of the future was revealed. In his dream Reinhard saw a map of Africa and on the map the name of one city — Johannesburg.

"I must confess that my geography of Africa was not too good in those days and when I awoke I immediately got out a map of Africa. What bothered me about the dream was the fact, that the city of Johannesburg seemed to be so far south. I was sure that it was nearer central Africa. But the Lord knows His geography, after all He designed this planet, and there was Johannesburg, exactly on the spot indicated in my dream," remembers Reinhard.

The dream, though, did not bring any dramatic change or any new course. Life went on as usual and Reinhard, eager to equip himself for the mission field, got a place at the Bible College of Wales. In fact, he confounded his parents and his local Pentecostal church, by insisting on going to this non-Pentecostal, conservative evangelical Bible college. Just as disturbing to the elders of the church in Krempe was the fact that Reinhard, now 19-years-old, couldn't speak English.

Despite his youth Reinhard revealed that he knew God's will for his life. He respected those who criticised him, but he refused to allow them to swerve him off his set course. Those who have had to deal closely with him over the years know this trait well. Easy-going on the surface and always willing to listen, but underneath it all is a steely determination to follow through once he has made a final decision. First impressions of that determination might be dismissed as a disguised form of stubbornness. And there have been men who have thought that about him — especially when he began to carve a place for himself in the African sun. Then later when he began to talk about multi-million Rand tents, some well-meaning Christians began to wag their heads. This determination, though, has obviously been the catalyst for a faith that is fearless in the face of any Goliath that would dare to taunt or challenge him.

So, undaunted, Reinhard packed his suitcase, stuffed his well-worn Bible in between his shirts and headed across the English Channel. Reinhard sometimes muses on this thought: why should God take a German; send him to a Bible College in Wales and then send him to be a missionary in Africa! It certainly sounds like a fruit salad.

# CHAPTER THREE

## Lessons in faith

The first three months at the Bible College were agony. He had taken it for granted that he would have to write all his examinations in English, not realising that he could have got a concession and written half of them in German, or not at all. But he fumbled, and struggled his way through the English language and, amazingly, after only three months he was preaching on weekend assignments without an interpreter.

But it wasn't easy. He would listen with great concentration to the lecturers and then at night he would go through his lessons by candlelight with a dictionary by his side trying to comprehend the English language. There were some advantages, though, to being unable to read English well. All the rules of the college were posted in English . . . but Reinhard couldn't read them and so he sometime or another broke every rule of the establishment.

Once he was severely reprimanded by a lecturer for filling his bath up to the brim — forbidden, of course, by a big notice on the bathroom door! Reinhard was relaxing in a beautiful, steaming bath, but unknown to him the overflow pipe was pouring out water into the courtyard above the main entrance to the men's hostel. Because of his foreign language he was able to speak in tongues without fellow students or lecturers being offended . They just believed he was praying in German!

His decision to attend the Welsh college was soon confirmed. As he went to lectures he realised just how little he really knew about the Word of God. New and wonderful truths began to unfold as he immersed himself in his studies.

One of the first things he discovered was that the staff all "lived by faith". This was something new to Reinhard, and his curiosity was aroused. None of the staff drew a pre-arranged salary. They received food and lodgings, but had to trust God for all their extras. As an example if the cook needed some new equipment in the kitchen she didn't put through a requisition form. Instead she prayed for it and trusted God to supply the item, whatever it was. To Reinhard's surprise it seemed to work and everybody seemed to be surviving. The staff prayed for their needs and when they received the answer they always used a phrase: "I've been delivered." It soon became the catch phrase of the students.

One day as the students gathered together in the dining room for a prayer meeting the principal came in. One of the rules of the prayer meeting was that no appeals were made known, except to God. The students were to prove for themselves that God answers prayer. This day when the principal came in he announced that £1 000 was needed by the end of the week to pay the bill for the coal. "I just want you to pray. We make no financial appeals."

That £1 000 was a lot of money in 1960 and Reinhard thought to himself: "Now let's see what happens."

At the end of the week the principal again attended

the prayer meeting and triumphantly proclaimed to the students: "Praise God, we've been delivered!

That incident rivetted Reinhard's attention on prayer and faith. From that moment he earnestly and sincerely began to pray: "Lord I want to be a man of faith, if you are prepared to trust me."

And so the seed of faith was planted in his spirit and immediately he decided to put it to the test. Up until then Reinhard had been well looked after financially by his parents and members of the church in Germany. He received parcels and money for his fees as well as pocket money. But now he began to seek God and yearn for this "real" faith. The Lord was dealing with him and the message was clear: "If you really want to become a man of faith, give away all the money you have. Give it to a missionary who passes through here and then you will see what I will do."

It was a challenge that Reinhard eagerly accepted, but tried to keep back £1, "just in case of an emergency." This brought a swift chiding from the Lord: "You see. You don't give me a chance to do a miracle. How can I do a miracle if you cater for yourself? You don't give Me a chance." It was a solemn moment as the quiet voice of the Spirit echoed in Reinhard's heart.

Reinhard saw that day the deep-seated, self-help programme that is in the human being and how people ingeniously look after themselves and by so doing cut out God, not giving Him half a chance to prove His power.

So Reinhard took the plunge in the faith pool and gave away all his money and although there may have been a few occasions when he felt that a tide of doubt would drown him, he progressively learned that to be a man of faith gained rich rewards, not just for himself, but for the Kingdom of God.

Thus he set out to experience this "faith thing" for himself. An opportunity arrived when he was given an assignment to speak at a Sunshine Corner meeting at the beachfront. All Reinhard had was half a crown in his pocket, the exact fare for a round trip by bus. But he wanted to take a friend along, a Dutch student named Tuinis.

So he went to Tuinis' room: "Tuin, let's go to the beach meeting together."

"I can't. I don't have any money," Tuinis replied.

"Well, I've got enough for two single tickets," said Reinhard.

"Yes, but how will we get back to the college?" asked Tuinis.

"Let's see what God can do for us. Let's trust Him. Let's ask Him to get us back," enthused Reinhard.

So the two young Bible students set off in high spirits and boarded the bus. The meeting was a success and the young people listened eagerly to the gospel stories. It was a beautiful day. The sea was calm and the children played happily on the beach while people strolled leisurely along the front. But Reinhard really didn't have much time to drink in the holiday atmosphere. All the while he was praying: "Lord, I need a half crown for our return fare. Lord, I am testing You now for the first time to see whether Your Word is true. I gave all my money away. It would have been easy for me to travel up and down, but I want to test You for the first time."

As he stood with his Dutch friend on the beachfront, they spotted a local pastor, a man they both knew. Immediately the thought flashed into Reinhard's mind: "Praise God, here comes our deliverance. If God can speak to anyone here on the beachfront, it must surely be this pastor because he is a man of God."

As the minister approached, the boys responded enthusiastically to his greeting and their faith soared when they were invited to join the pastor for a cup of tea in a nearby restaurant overlooking the beach. As they sat together sipping tea, swopping stories and listening to the pastor relating some of his experiences, Reinhard's prayer lifeline to Heaven was pulsing out a constant SOS: "Lord, just a half a crown. Speak to this man. Just a half a crown!"

Hoping to provoke the situation, Reinhard spoke up: "Our bus is coming soon. We can't stay too long." So the minister called for the waitress and paid the bill. On-lookers must have thought the boys very rude as they stared at the minister while he paid the bill . . . inside the man's purse were several half crowns . . . surely he'd realise their need!

"Well, it's been nice meeting you boys. Keep up the studies." They shook hands. And that was it. No money.

Reinhard looked rather glumly at Tuin and they dragged their feet along as they walked to the bus stop. Black clouds of doubt began to hover over Reinhard's spirit. He so much wanted to see God provide, but now . . . As his mind and spirit wrestled with the situation he was suddenly conscious of someone running behind them. They turned and an elderly lady, handbag swaying on her arm, and a bit out of breath, almost bowled them over.

"Boys," she said, fumbling with her bag and

reaching for her purse, "I liked your little message so much. Here, take this."

She pushed forward her hand and two gleaming half crowns dropped into Reinhard's palm. Five shillings! Reinhard and his friend beamed broadly at each other. "Praise God. Lord you are faithful." They rushed off rejoicing and as he paid the fare at the ticket office, Reinhard marvelled at God's goodness as the half crown slid across the counter. Inside his money pocket he could feel the warm glow of the other half crown. Surely, these coins had been minted in Heaven!

That was his first genuine answer to prayer on the royal road of faith. The "deliverance" had not come from the source he had expected and right there Reinhard learned a major lesson in living by faith. Never count on what may look to be the obvious way out. Also never look to rich people and think that because they are wealthy they will supply the financial needs.

Studies continued as normal and his English improved — he knew that because now he could read the rules! The lecturers at the college were not just interested in filling the students' minds with Bible knowledge. They were concerned in shaping character. And part of that meant breaking the proud self. But the 60-odd students were constantly inspired by the example of the staff.

His missionary zeal grew and the faith life enchanted him. He soon came to realise that for faith to grow it had to be exercised, otherwise it would shrivel up. One couldn't stay at the half crown level all of one's life!

One day while praying God spoke clearly into

Reinhard's spirit instructing him to return to Germany on holiday when the next college recess came.

Now here was a challenge to his faith. He had no money at all, but went into Swansea and found a travel agent on Wind Street and made a booking. A few days before he was due to leave, the travel agency telephoned and asked him to come in and collect his ticket. He still didn't have a penny to his name. Stalling them off, Reinhard told them: "I will come in time. Don't worry."

With the deadline nearing, Reinhard was spending much time on his knees. "Lord, you told me to give all my money away. Now You are telling me to go to Germany. You've got to supply my need. I'm not telling anybody about it."

The days passed and the day before he was due to depart Reinhard was again on his knees. "You only have one more chance. Tomorow morning before nine o'clock I must find the money on the letter board. That is Your last chance. I see no other way. Please, Lord Jesus!"

The next morning Reinhard could hardly keep still. He raced through breakfast and paced restlessly up and down the corridors and in the beautiful Italian gardens that surrounded the college buildings. His whole being was focused on one thing: the money for the ticket.

At nine o'clock he ran to the letter board. Yes, there was a letter and it was addressed to him. His heart began to beat faster as he ripped it open . . . this must be it. His hands were quivering as he pulled and tugged to get at the contents of the letter expecting, of course, that a cheque would come fluttering out. But what a disappointment. The letter was nothing more than a routine circular. He felt as though an ice cold bucket of water had been poured over him as he stood staring blankly at the worthless piece of paper in his hand.

But inside of him something seemed to be saying 'hang on'. Trying to hide his disappointment Reinhard walked quickly back across the courtyard and up to his room. There was only one last resort — pray again!

As he knelt at his bed, he heard Tuin at the door and asked him to come and join him. While they prayed the travel agency telephoned again. An urgent voice crackled over the receiver: "Mr Bonnke when are you coming to collect your ticket? Your train leaves at one o'clock."

Reinhard stood there, looking across at Tuinis and then took a deep breath and said as calmly as he could: "Don't worry, I will come and collect it in time." As he replaced the telephone receiver his words echoed in his mind . . . "Don't worry . . . " His suitcase was packed. His ticket was booked, everything was ready — but he didn't have a penny to his name. He could hardly believe the reality of the situation as he walked away from the telephone and went back to praying. Again he cried "Lord, You told me to give my money away. You told me to go to Germany. Now I am testing you. You promised, but time is running out."

Ten thirty came, then 11 o'clock. Then Reinhard turned to his friend and said: "Let's go to one of the classrooms and there we can shout to God." So off they went and walking up and down in one of the empty classrooms they began to pray out loudly. While they prayed the words of a chorus suddenly came to Reinhard's lips. It was one they often sung:

"There's nothing too hard for Thee
There's nothing too hard for Thee.
Nothing, nothing,
There's nothing too hard for Thee.

I'm trusting alone in Thee
I'm trusting alone in Thee;
Trusting, trusting,
I'm trusting alone in Thee

It's never too late for Thee Dear Lord
It's never too late for Thee;
Never, never,
It's never too late for Thee."

As they sang the last verse Reinhard experienced something which even today he finds difficult to explain. That little mustard seed of faith that he had clung onto seemed to grow and grow. It was as though he entered a new dimension. It was a calm, Divine assurance that all was well.

With the words of the verse still vibrating in the classroom, Reinhard jumped to his feet and exclaimed: "The money is there!" A bewildered Tuinis looked up at him and asked the leading question: "Where?" Back came the sublime answer: "I don't know, but I know it is there!"

They jumped up together and raced across the garden to the hostel. As they rounded a big hedge a man came running toward them. He was a tall man and he stopped when he saw them. Breathing heavily he looked straight at Reinhard and asked: "How much money do you need?''. Reinhard stared at him for a moment. This was it! "God knows the amount. I'm not telling you."

The man dug into his pockets and stuffed a handful of notes into Reinhard's hands. "There," he said and before Reinhard could say anything further the man left.

For a moment Reinhard stood as though in a dream world. But the feel of the bank notes in his hands confirmed that he was not dreaming. He counted the money, with Tuinis checking. It was the exact amount needed for the fare. Dashing to his room Reinhard grabbed his suitcase and ran for a bus. In town he charged into the travel office, paid for the ticket and then started on another wild chase to the station. The travel agent had told him the train would be leaving in 15 minutes. There was no way he was going to miss that train — not after the way God had provided the money.

He must have looked like a marathon runner at the end of a race as he barged onto the platform. The final bell had sounded and the wheels of the train were slowly grinding on the rails as Reinhard flung open a door and piled in to the moving train. He flopped onto the nearest seat, exhausted physically, but inside his spirit was rejoicing.

Now he knew beyond any doubt — God answered prayer and if he could provide for an unknown German Bible student in Britain, then He would provide for him when he eventually went to Africa!

After two years Reinhard successfully passed his examinations and with Bible and diploma under arm the fresh-faced young Reinhard was ready to win the world for Jesus, or more explicitly, Africa. But the gateway to Africa was barred.

God restrained the zeal and led him into evangelistic work in Germany. It was here that he got his first taste of crusade work and of preaching in tents. Standing under the canvas canopies preaching the gospel to fellow Germans, he little knew that tents would become the trademark of one of the world's most anointed and dynamic gospel outreaches.

When Reinhard moved to Flensburg, in northern Germany, and pioneered a church with the help of a collegue, it seemed that the dream of going to Africa was fading. Especially when he met a young lady, Anni, who was to become his wife and the Bonnke's settled down to a modest church routine. In 1966 a son, Freddy, was born.

Yet Africa tugged at his heart. He would not lose the vision, and obviously God would not let him go. But when he announced to his thriving congregation that he was going to Africa they were dismayed.

Some mused at what they thought was bravado. The majority begged and pleaded for him to stay, but there was no way anything or anyone was going to stop him from going to Africa. It was once again that steely determination that marks his decision making. He was going because he believed this was God's time and nothing and nobody was going to stand in his way. His mind was set. At last, after eight years, Africa was in his sights. He could already visualise the grass huts and feel the burning sun. No soppy sentiment was going to dissuade him from fulfilling his life's calling. Africa was waiting.

# CHAPTER FOUR

## Blanket of death

His first year in southern Africa was almost a disaster. He worked in Ermelo, where their second child, a daughter named Gabi was born. Reinhard had come to Africa with his own ideas about how a missionary should operate. One of the things that Reinhard cherished was freedom and he did not take kindly to the shackles of mission boards.

However, he had to grit his teeth firmly and tighten his belt. Because Reinhard is a man loath to criticise he doesn't talk much about his first year on the mission field. He learned to submit to his superiors although he disagreed with some of their methods. He wanted to get out and preach to the African people, but his superiors felt that he needed to be gently eased into the new conditions and also needed time to learn and observe the many strange traditions and way of life of the African people.

He desperately wanted to fly from the cage that he felt he had been trapped in and he began to eye the independent nation of Swaziland. Then he got an opportunity to visit Maseru, capital of the mountain kingdom of Lesotho. What he saw there touched him. Lesotho, once the British Protectorate of Basutuland was a poor, landlocked country. The people lived off the land and there was very little industrialisation. Hundreds of thousands of young Basuto men travel each year to work on the gold mines of South Africa, bringing home good pay packets and luxury items. "There was a spirit of helplessness about the place," he recalls, and that night, after returning from Maseru, there was a restlessness in his spirit when he closed his eyes. He knew inside of him that he had to make a move. He could not stay any longer in South Africa. He had to move − or perish. But where to? He wanted desperately to make the move that pleased God. He did not want to deviate from the Sovereign Will. He wanted to stay within the bounds of the plan that God had drawn for his life.

Next morning, while reading his Bible, Reinhard came across a passage in Judges that seemed to leap up at his eyes. Not only did the scripture seem to indicate Lesotho, but it also promised the blessing to accomplish the job God wanted him to do in that poor, neglected country.

Arrangements were made with his mission board and he got the green light from his superiors, who obviously had faith in this enthusiastic German missionary, who had such a burning zeal to preach the gospel to the people of Africa. He was thrilled to be given the opportunity by the AFM executive. Often he had felt like a Samson, shorn of his hair, but now he was going to be given the opportunity to flex his muscles. For a year he'd had to stand patiently in the wings, now the call had come and he was ready to step out onto the stage of the rugged, mountain country of Lesotho.

The move to Lesotho was not immediate as they lived at Ladybrand, a small farming town in the province of the Orange Free State. It is just across the border from Lesotho. But once their third child, Susi was born, in May 1969, they moved to Maseru to live among the people they were working with.

Lesotho gave Reinhard his freedom and for the next six years he worked tirelessly at evangelising Lesotho. They were hard, tough years. The children were growing up — his son Freddy went to the local school and when looking back at Lesotho, Reinhard would probably call them the lean years of his ministry. Despite all his efforts, preaching from village to village; building a fine church in the capital city of Maseru, starting a Bible correspondence course that reached thousands of people, not only in Lesotho, but in other countries of Africa, Reinhard was still not satisfied.

And that I suppose is the dynamo that hums within his spirit. He wants to achieve and is a perfectionist. Deep inside of him beats a heart that is always striving for more and more of God's grace. He deliberately wants to delve into God's limitless supply.

Although he may not say it, Reinhard loves a challenge. At heart he is an adventurer. A man who will dare anything for God — no matter how difficult the task. And so while other missionaries might have boasted of success, Reinhard looked at the Lesotho scene with criticial eyes. He examined the work and examined himself and came to a staggering conclusion: it was not good enough. There had to be another challenge. There had to be something bigger to tackle. What would it be? Only God knew, but he was willing to risk all by leaving Lesotho and heading for Johannesburg.

Yes, somewhere in his spirit that dream still glowed. Johannesburg. If that dream he had experienced as a teenager was from God, then he must go to Johannesburg — the city of gold. But before then Reinhard had a close brush with death.

Carelessly he had drunk some water without boiling it first. It had been a blazing hot day, with hardly a cloud in the sky and he had been driving along the twisting, dusty mountain roads visiting some local pastors. He arrived at a small village by the name of Kolonyama. His throat was parched and he felt as though he had trekked across the Sahara desert. The offer of a cool drink of water was like stumbling into a green-fringed oasis. He gulped down the water.

That night in Maseru he fell violently ill. At first he thought it was a bout of dysentery. But by the next morning he was desperately ill. He lay in his bed exhausted, slipping into fits of delirium. At his bedside his wife prayed and the message went out to his fellow African pastors: "The Moruti is sick. Pray for him."

The fever raged and he got steadily weaker and weaker. He was unable to eat and he was fast losing contact with what was going on around him.

On the third day he experienced a strange vision. His eyes were wide open and he saw a blanket, a black blanket floating down towards him. It wanted to cover him. Instinctively he knew what the blanket meant: death. Suddenly he found that he could see through the blanket and on the other side there was a face — the face of the Lord Jesus. Despite his delirious condition a soothing comfort came over him when he gazed into His face. Then something even more strange happened. He was suddenly conscious of someone praying. Someone agonizing in soul, crying, pleading with God . . . begging and praying for his life. He knew the voice. It was that of Mrs Eliese Köhler, a dear, loyal and devoted member of his father's church in Germany.

As he listened to her praying the blanket began to fade away and Reinhard recalls that he slipped off into a quiet, restful sleep. The red hot fever that seared his body subsided. The crisis was over and Reinhard would live to preach another sermon.

It took him many weeks to recover, but when he did he wrote a letter to his father and asked him to contact Mrs Köhler and ask her what had happened to her on the day he had seen the "death blanket".

His father's reply confirmed what Reinhard already believed had happened. Sister Köhler had risen early that morning and had been urged by the Holy Spirit to pray for Reinhard. As she prayed so the burden for Reinhard intensified until she realised that she was interceding for his very life. She spent virtually the whole day praying for him. To Reinhard it underlined once again the mighty power of prayer. Here a woman had prayed in Germany 10 000 km away from where the need was and God had dramatically acted because of the faithfulness and obedience of one woman. Whenever Reinhard utters a prayer it is never just an idle disseration for he has experienced the potency of prayer on many occasions.

# CHAPTER FIVE

## Chariot of fire

While in Lesotho two further incidents of note are worth recording. Both are linked and were once again a drawing back of Heaven's curtain for God to supernaturally intervene in Reinhard's ministry. The one incident still makes him blush to this day. It involved a financial deal that went wrong. In fact, Reinhard was taken for a ride and paid dearly for it in hard cash.

He had hired two offices in the 60-Minute Dry Cleaner Building in Maseru. It was a very plain office and the walls so thin that one could hear the conversation quite plainly in the office next door.

Across the dingy hall was a business selling furniture from catalogues, and some of the African pastors came and asked Reinhard to help them buy some furniture. Reinhard's salary in 1970 was R110 a month. Survival was about the best word he could use in those days.

The pastors kept pressuring him each time they visited him in the offices. "We can get a dining room suite for only R50. Can't you help us?", they pleaded.

"I was really put on the spot. I knew the poor conditions the pastors lived in. In most instances old, discarded items made up the bulk of their household furniture. So I prayed: 'Lord Jesus you said we should not close our hearts. I'm going to do something I've never done before in my life. I'm going to borrow money and lend it to these pastors, my dear brothers.'"

And so he raised some money and the pastors went off and ordered furniture to the value of R475. When the pastors told him how much furniture they had ordered he became suspicious and asked the furniture salesman how he could sell the furniture so cheaply? Was it stolen? The man assured him that all was well and so the contracts were signed and the money was paid over in advance.

Four weeks later the furniture deal exploded. The furniture was being bought on hire purchase agreements across the border in South Africa and the sale of the goods in Lesotho was illegal.

In his office that evening Reinhard received a telephone call from one of his African ministers, Pastor Mphosi, informing him that the furniture salesman was going to skip across the border. "Please stop him. Get a lawyer otherwise we are going to lose everything," pleaded the pastor. As Reinhard put down the telephone, his spirits low, he wondered which lawyer he should contact. Then slowly he bowed his head and prayed: "Lord Jesus, You are my Lawyer. I put this case in Your hands."

Next morning when he returned to his office Pastor Mphosi was waiting.

"Have you seen a lawyer? he asked.

"Yes," replied Reinhard.

"Which one?"

"The best in town."

After a pause the pastor asked: "Who is that?"

"Jesus," smiled Reinhard.

Reinhard recalls that the man's face did not show much emotion at that statement. "I think he was disappointed, but I was resting my case with Jesus."

The furniture man skipped the country and the pastors never got their furniture, but two weeks later Reinhard was invited to speak at some special meetings. He had told no one about his unfortunate loss – he honestly felt ashamed about the incident. After one of the services a man came up to him and pressed an envelope into his hand, telling him that it was a gift for his own personal use. When he opened it up he was astonished to find that it was the exact amount that he had lost on the furniture transaction and he was able to pay back the loan that he had taken. As he quipped later: "The wonderful thing about this is that my Lawyer charges no fees!"

The second incident also involved finance, but this experience came from a very different angle. It is best explained in Reinhard's own words:

"I was driving through the flat, almost treeless Free State on my way to Bloemfontein. The Bible correspondence course had been going for five years now and we had an enrolment of 50 000. But it was a costly business to keep it running and I was always scratching around to get some extra finance to keep the courses going.

"To save costs I bought envelopes in bulk – 100 000 at a time, but I had to wait until I had saved enough cash before I ordered them. As my well-worn Mercedes diesel-engined car pounded along the tar my mind was reflecting on that unhappy furniture deal I had become involved in.

"Lord, there is one thing I will never be able to understand. If I had borrowed that money to enrich myself, then I could understand why you allowed me to fall into that pit. Lord Jesus you know better than anybody else that I borrowed that money to help the poorest of the poor. I did it for Your Word's sake. I did it for my brother's sake. Lord, I cannot understand why you allowed this to happen.'

"What happened next is hard to describe. Suddenly Jesus was tangibly in that old car. It was as if that old Mercedes car became a flaming chariot. It filled with the glory and presence of God. Tears gushed out of my eyes and I thought I was in Heaven. The spiritual fulfilment I experienced that moment cannot be put into words. I was no longer conscious of steering the vehicle or of the passing scenery. I felt as though I was being wrapped up in God's glory and being posted to Heaven. The thoughts of the furniture money disappeared and then I heard a voice say: 'The flour in the box shall not diminish and the oil in the cruse shall not become less.'

"Then the glory lifted and to my amazement I saw that my old car was still pointed in the direction of Bloemfontein! As I regained my composure the words began ringing in my heart: 'The flour in the box will not diminish and the oil in the cruse shall not grow less.'

"I knew what it meant. I had two mission accounts at the bank. 'All right Lord my two accounts . . . one is the box and the other is the cruse. My duty is to pour them out. Your job is to fill them up.' That was in 1970 and I have never managed to get into the red with the work that God has sent me to do in Africa. I have sometimes overspent, only to find that the amount was met by some unknown deposit."

That sacred, heavenly experience happened 14

years ago and there is no doubt that Reinhard has pushed hard to empty the barrel. Sometimes his bookkeeper has thrown up his arms in despair when accounts have fluttered on the desk like confetti, but somehow, they all get paid. Sometimes it's been like walking a tight rope. Not that Reinhard is reckless when it comes to finance. Neither is he extravagant. I have heard him state on several occasions that he is prepared to sell all his wordly goods for the sake of the gospel. I've also noticed his wife Anni raise her eyebrows when he makes such statements! Because of his strong determination to get a divine task done he sometimes strains the purse strings. In later years when the Big Tent eventually came into production it proved a tremendous financial drain on the whole of his organisation. The men working on the tent demanded more and more equipment and Reinhard could not turn a deaf ear. The Big Tent got preferential treatment. This, of course, led to some frustration because other outreach work was forced to take a back seat. But despite the financial pressures Reinhard always manages to sail serenely through them. Others get agitated and concerned, but somehow one gets the feeling that all is well, so long as Reinhard is out there preaching. His coolness in the middle of a cash crisis must surely be traced back to that supernatural encounter on a lonely stretch of road in the Free State.

# CHAPTER SIX

## Just a missionary

Now followed an event which totally re-shaped Reinhard's ministry. In fact, it was almost like having Moses' rod slapped into his hand or having the mantle of Elijah slide over his back. It signalled the beginning of a new ministry, but when it happened it looked like a disaster. In fact, Reinhard almost visualised himself being stoned at the city gates!

In many ways Reinhard was just one more missionary toiling away under the scorching African sun. People got saved, people were baptised, but it was a continuous struggle. As Reinhard recalls: "Everybody said Lesotho was a difficult place. I agreed heartily with them and that's what I kept saying. Little did I realise that I was snaring myself with those words. I prayed earnestly for a major breakthrough, but I became even more convinced that "this place is too difficult". When we got 50 people at a service it was like Heaven had come to earth. I thought the great outpouring had begun!"

Deep inside, however, he longed for something bigger. Something greater. Something that would bring resounding praise to God. Something that would shake people out of their lethargy. Something that would demonstrate that Jesus is alive. Something that would cause men and women to come to the

Saviour in large numbers.

With this in mind he invited a well-known evangelist, who also had an anointed healing ministry to preach at two services. The man was to minister on the Saturday night and on the Sunday morning.

Reinhard and his helpers were wildly enthusiastic. The printing press was running furiously to get out handbills and posters. They even managed to get some time on the local radio station. The posters told about cripples walking and the blind seeing. Reinhard's faith was higher than Mount Zion as the time for the crusade drew near. It was the talk of the town and when Reinhard walked into his church on the Saturday night it was packed. He rejoiced and felt sure that the breakthrough he had been praying for would come at last. Now the superstitious minds of those who trusted in witchcraft would see what the Lord Jesus Christ could do.

As Reinhard stood on the platform, looking over the sea of faces he felt a tingle at the back of his neck. He had never seen so many people in the building before. And as he glanced over the crowd he was touched as the lame limped down the aisle looking for a place to sit and at some twisted human forms that dragged themselves along on all fours to get into the church building. The sight of those mangled, twisted limbs moved his heart. Oh! to see these people healed by the power of God, was the sigh of his heart as the chatter of the crowd was replaced by the harmony of African voices singing hymns.

The meeting began. The evangelist preached well, but the atmosphere was just not right. Hardly anything happened. In fact, halfway through the service the evangelist turned to Reinhard and urged him to close the meeting. Reinhard was flabbergasted. "I cannot do that. These people want you to pray for them."

"No, close, the meeting," argued the evangelist.

Reinhard's mind was in a turmoil. Hundreds of eyes stared at the two preachers waiting. . . hoping.

"All right, I'll close the meeting, but you must promise to pray for them tomorrow morning." The evangelist agreed and the meeting was closed.

As he turned off the lights and locked the church doors Reinhard's heart was sad. Everything seemed right for a revival. Just one look at the faces of the people could have told anyone that. As he slipped into bed that night a little air of apprehension nestled into his heart. But surely things would be better tomorrow morning, he thought.

Sunday morning dawned. Reinhard rose and briskly washed and shaved before going to where the evangelist was staying. To his amazement he found him in his safari suit, with his suitcase packed and about to climb into a waiting car.

"What's happening?" demanded Reinhard.

"I'm going home."

"No you can't do that. You dare not. I have just come from the church. It's full — there are more people than last night. You cannot go."

There was a note of despair in Reinhard's voice. How could this man just desert him with the church full and everybody waiting for him to pray for them?

The evangelist turned and faced Reinhard, looking him straight in the eyes: "The Holy Spirit told me I must go."

Reinhard checked himself. This was different. "If

the Holy Spirit told you to go then you have no option. You must go. You dare not disobey the Holy Spirit. God bless you. Goodbye."

Reinhard watched the evangelist drive off down the road then climbed back into his own car. He was upset as he cried to God: "I am not a big name preacher, I am just a missionary, one of Your little men, but now I will preach at this meeting and You will do the miracles."

Then in utter desperation Reinhard drove to the church, sliding to a halt in a cloud of dust. There was nothing else for him to do. He would have to preach, and muttering a prayer under his breath, he called his African pastors together and told them what had happened. Gloom settled over them. But he ignored their attempts to protest. "I am going to preach and God is going to do the miracles," he told them with a boldness that even surprised himself.

Bible firmly clasped in his hand he strode up on the platform. He knew what was going through each one of those minds. Each pair of eyes asked the same question: "Where is the great man of God?" Looking straight at the audience Reinhard told them the evangelist had left. He held his breath. What would the congregation do? There was a shuffling in the front row. Two men got up and walked out. Would that be the signal for a mass exodus? No, as the two men pushed their way through the crowd others began elbowing their way to the front, eager to gain a vantage point. The rest of the audience sat . . . waiting.

Reinhard began to preach. And as he did an anointing of the Holy Spirit fell upon the people. Never before had he experienced the power of God with such intensity. In fact, it became quite comical when his interpreter broke down in the middle of the message, sinking to the floor with tears flowing from his eyes — because of the holy presence and power of God in the hall. It was a strange sight, though. There was Reinhard, arms waving as he stressed his point, and on the floor lay the interpreter!

Pausing for the interpreter to get up and regain his composure Reinhard heard "words" that not only made his ears tingle, but almost left him speechless. As he stood there he heard: "My Words in your mouth are just as powerful as My Words in My own mouth."

His senses reeled and then the "voice" repeated the sentence. Then, Reinhard recalls, like a movie film he "saw" the power of the Word of God. God spoke and it happened. Jesus had told his disciples to speak to the sycamore tree and it would finish up in the sea.

"I suddenly realised that the power was not in the mouth — the power was in the Word."

The interpreter, in the meantime, had regained his feet and Reinhard continued his message and then again the voice of the Holy Spirit prompted him: "Call those who are completely blind and speak the Word of Authority." Hardly daring to believe what he was "hearing" and hardly daring to disobey he called out to the congregation: "How many totally blind people do we have here?" About half a dozen people stood up.

Meanwhile, on the platform Reinhard began to have second thoughts about what he was doing. "I remember the devil dropping this thought into my mind: 'What happens if nothing happens?' But then I whispered under my breath: 'I'm going to do what Jesus told me to do.'

As the blind people stood next to their seats the jabber of the people ceased. All eyes were on the minister. Reinhard knew this would be a moment of truth — for him and for the congregation. He turned and looked at the faces of the poor, blind people standing before him and boldly proclaimed: "Now I am going to speak with the authority of God and you are going to see a White man standing before you. Your eyes are going to open."

It could have been a modern-day Mount Carmel duel with the servant of God poised to call down the fire to consume the sacrifice and the water as the prophets of Baal looked on. Surrounded as he was by Africans who were firm believers in the powers of witchcraft, Reinhard knew that it was not his reputation that was at stake.

Taking a deep breath Reinhard shouted: "In the Name of Jesus, blind eyes open!" The power of his voice jolted even those on the stage. It felt as though a flaming bolt of lightning was let loose in the building. His voice was still resonanting against the bare brick walls when there was another shout. This time it was the shriek of a woman's voice. What she screamed shattered the silence that hung over the congregation: "I can see! I can see!"

A woman, who had been totally blind for four years, jumped forward toward Reinhard. Almost out of control she grabbed people around her demonstrating that she could see. Now the congregation began to shout. There was bedlam in the church. A woman fought and pushed her way through the seething mass of bodies. Standing before the microphone she declared: "Whether you believe it or not, I can see. Give me something to read. I can see again.''

It sounded more like a football crowd on cup final day as cheers erupted through the building. A young woman with a crippled child in her arms tried to get to the front. She couldn't get through the crowd which jammed the way up to the platform so she handed the boy over her head and he was passed on until a frail little body was thrust into Reinhard's outstretched arms.

As the child lay helpless in his arms Reinhard prayed and then sensed a surge of God's power through the child's body. He saw the child's legs begin to vibrate. Amazed at what he was seeing Reinhard put the little boy down on the platform. It was like putting a wound-up clockwork toy on the floor. The boy stood for a moment, then started to run. His crippled legs straightened before everyone's eyes. He just ran to the right and to the left. The screaming and shouting of the people made it sound like torrents of mighty waters.

The meeting continued for several hours. There was no way that Reinhard could close the meeting. He and his co-pastors prayed for countless numbers of people that morning and the singing filled the church with praise. Jesus was alive and the people of Maseru knew it beyond any doubt on that glorious Sunday morning.

When the meeting ended and the last few people had left one man remained behind. He walked quietly into a darkened corner of the empty church, bowed his head and with folded hands prayed: ''Thank you, Holy Spirit for sending the big evangelist away. Thank you because now nobody can say it was him. Everybody is saying it was Jesus who did the miracles.

This is how I want to serve you. This is how I want to work with you."

Reinhard Bonnke had entered a new dimension. He had tasted honey and no longer would he be satisfied with syrup!

That, incident more than any other, encouraged him to quit Lesotho. He knew that God had commissioned him with a better and more authoritative ministry. Like Moses retreated into the desert and then returned to be God's mighty instrument to deliver the Jews from Egypt, so the zealous young German missionary was ready to come in from the wilderness of Lesotho into the Promised Land, which in this case was very specifically a city by the name of Johannesburg.

# CHAPTER SEVEN

## A million souls

Reinhard visited South Africa on several occasions during the last quarter of 1974 for discussions with the Apostolic Faith Mission executive on prospects for moving to Johannesburg.

In Maseru the Lord was shaking lose the roots that Reinhard had put down in Lesotho. One day, while walking home and despairing over how he was going to pay his office rent he heard the Lord speak clearly into his heart: "Do you want me to give you R1-million?" Reinhard stopped in his tracks. What a wonderful thought . . . he naively believed at that moment that he could win the world if he had that much cash.

Then something stirred deep in his soul and ignoring the passersby in the street, he lifted his hands in the air and with tears in his eyes he cried out: "No, Lord, don't give me a R1-million, give me a million souls. A million souls plucked out of hell's jaws. A million souls for heaven." Out of this encounter came Reinhard's now famous war cry: "Let's plunder hell and populate heaven."

If that phrase was to become a reality then he knew that he had to move, and so in October 1974 the Bonnkes visited the AFM headquarters at Maranatha Park, with a view to finalising their move and finding a new home. While being driven around some of the suburbs they passed through the East Rand town of Boksburg, which is about 20 km east of Johannesburg. They passed through one of the town's suburbs, called Witfield, and spotted some new houses. All, except one, were already sold. Recalling that day Anni Bonnke said: "I didn't like any of the other houses, the unsold house was the one I wanted." With little waste of time the house was purchased and the Bonnke family moved in just before Christmas 1974. They've been living in the same house since that time.

The significance of the move to Witfield was quite striking because when Reinhard got the "call" to leave Lesotho and head for Johannesburg the Holy Spirit clearly indicated to him to establish his headquarters close to Jan Smuts, South Africa's international airport. Witfield is less than 10 minutes away from Jan Smuts Airport by car and as God's plan unfolded further, Christ for all Nations' offices are now situated a mere three kilometres away from the Bonnke's home.

However, the tensions of the past few months took a heavy toll on Reinhard's health. Never a man to nurse himself, he often drives himself dangerously near to his physical limit. For several weeks before leaving Maseru Anni noticed a strange lethargy about her husband. The usual zest for life was not there. She put it down to the coming move and hoped that he would regain his old zeal once they were settled in their new house in Witfield. But the malady lingered and Reinhard had to confess that he was a sick man. It was hard to accept for a man who proclaimed a message that not only saved people from their sin, but also delivered them from sickness. And it was not just an academic preaching of divine healing — he had seen miracles happen with his own eyes. Now he was ill and his prayers didn't appear to be getting any answers.

"I was very sick. I didn't think I would make it. I went to doctors. Nothing helped. I was crying to God: 'Lord what are you doing? What is your plan?' One afternoon I retired to my study. A thirst for prayer came over me and I was hardly on my knees when I saw a most wonderful vision. I saw the Son of God stand in front of me in full armour, like a general. The armour was shining like the sun and burning like fire. It was tremendous and I realised that the Lord of Hosts had come. I threw myself at His feet. I laughed and I cried . . . I don't know for how long, but when I got up I was perfectly healed," remembers Reinhard. That was early in January 1975 and this was going to prove to be a momentous year in his life.

He was to initiate an extraordinary gospel outreach to the sprawling Black township of Soweto, next to Johannesburg, and more importantly Christ for all Nations would be officially launched.

Because his Home Mission Board would not always back some of his projects, Reinhard realised that if he wanted to see his own initiative succeed he would need an outside source of cash. So while in Lesotho he had gained private support for some of his own projects and to avoid any financial queries and to ensure his integrity, he had kept separate accounts. This account was run under the name of Christ for all Nations, or CFAN as it is popularly known throughout Africa. The name had actually been registered in 1972, but it was the year 1975 that saw CFAN in banner-size letters for the first time as it became the name under which Reinhard Bonnke would campaign in a ministry that would reach the four corners of the earth.

# CHAPTER EIGHT

## Botswana breakthrough

Always quick to seize opportunities Reinhard had been involved in a gospel radio outreach and his programmes had been broadcast by Radio Lesotho. Response from these programmes had always been encouraging. He had travelled to Accra in Ghana, to Lusaka, Zambia, and to Swaziland to buy time for his gospel messages and to advertise his Bible correspondence courses. Tens of thousands of people took these courses, and there was the continuous thrill of getting letters telling of how people had come to know Jesus as their personal Saviour. There was one remarkable testimony from a man in Lusaka, Zambia. He wrote that he had decided to commit suicide and had driven his car to a lonely spot, planning to gas himself by running a hose from the exhaust pipe into his car. He then sat back with the engine running, ready to die, but obviously thinking that some music might cheer him up as he slipped into eternity, switched on his car radio. Soon the man was captivated by what he heard as the voice of Reinhard Bonnke filled his car and challenged him to repent and make Jesus his Saviour. The man did just that, quickly dismantling his suicide hosepipe and driving home to tell his family of his new friend − Jesus!

So he was acutely aware of the importance of gospel radio time and with this in view he began to search for new outlets. This decision became the gateway to something more thrilling and dynamic. He turned his attention to Botswana, another landlocked neighbour of South Africa's which also borders on Namibia, Zambia and Zimbabwe. It's a desolate country, made up mostly of the harsh Kalahari desert and famous for the little bushmen, who survive by the most primitive means in this hostile environment. But Botswana boasted a radio station that beamed into many neighbouring countries and with the intention of getting time on this station Reinhard flew off to the capital of Gaborone.

As the plane banked over Gaborone, Reinhard stared down at the landscape and almost everywhere he looked was a monotonous brown and then a patch of green caught his eye just before the plane made its approach to land — it was the Botswana National Sports Stadium. But it meant nothing to him. Sport didn't interest him, but little did he realise then, that sports stadiums were going to become an arena for his preaching of the gospel.

Strolling along the sidewalk in the blazing morning sun, he found himself going past the National Sports Stadium. To use his own words he was "rooted to the ground" when suddenly the voice of the Holy Spirit spoke clearly to him:"I want you to preach my Word there." Keenly aware that this was not something he was making up and that it was the Holy Spirit speaking to him he quickly responded with: "Lord, you said it and I am going to do it. I have always wanted to preach in a stadium, I believe you."

Inside, Reinhard's spirit surged like a giant ocean wave, trapped within a rocky cove. He sensed that this was not just a fleeting feeling of joy. No, this was something different. This, in fact, could be the reason for God calling him out of Lesotho. Forgetting the hot sun that caused him to screw up his eyes because of the bright glare, Reinhard reached his destination in the city and was soon having a discussion with a local pastor.

Negotiations for radio time was no longer a priority. He got hold of Pastor Scheffers and told him he was going to hold a city-wide crusade. The pastor became excited, but when Reinhard asked to make arrangements to hire the National Sports Stadium, there was a cool silence and obvious doubt etched the man's face. He may well have thought that the German brother was suffering from a touch of the sun! But Reinhard repeated his request, asking that in the meantime the city hall be hired so as to start the campaign.

The pastor scratched his head and as politely as he could told Reinhard that he was obviously unware of the local situation. "Why, I only get 40 people to a service on a Sunday morning. And you're talking about hiring the stadium . . . and a hall. Surely, brother. . ."

Reinhard, displaying what to some may have appeared presumptuous faith, didn't even allow the local pastor to finish his sentence. His mind was made up: "Hire the biggest hall in town, also make arrangements to get the use of the sports stadium and I'll be back in 30 days with a team."

He concluded his business and then flew directly back to Johannesburg to organize a crusade team for Gaborone. His heart was full of expectancy. In his mind's eyes he could already see himself preaching in the national sports stadium.

Rushing around and using his contacts in the AFM, Reinhard got together a small team of workers with Pastor Richard Ngidi, the key man. He was a big, lovable middle-aged Zulu man who would act as co-evangelist. Reinhard knew Ngidi and had been keen to work with him for he was a man used by God and greatly respected. However, Reinhard was wary about making any approaches to him for fear that fellow colleagues might think he was poaching in their territory. So for this reason, Reinhard refrained from asking Pastor Ngidi straight out to join him for the Gaborone crusade. Instead he prayed.

A few days later Reinhard attended a youth conference and as he walked into the hall he spotted Pastor Ngidi, who called him over. He told Reinhard that he wanted to work with him and so the first Christ for all Nations team was complete when they set off for Gaborone in April 1975.

The campaign had been publicised in the press and posters had been placed all over the town and the local pastor had worked feverishly to herd up as many people as possible, collecting them in cars and bringing them to the city hall.

The opening night of the crusade arrived and when Reinhard stood up to preach he looked down at 100 faces. The hall looked very empty. It had seating for 800 and the stadium 10 000!

The local pastor, though, was thrilled. But he warned Reinhard that he couldn't expect the crowds to get any bigger, because all of his congregation of 40 people were at this service. There just weren't anymore people he could bring!

Here, of course, was an opportunity for him to show his greatness as a man who trusts God. He could have faltered at this hurdle, but he believed with all his heart that God had spoken to him outside the football stadium — and if it was God then He would bless the campaign. Reinhard's faith had been maturing over the years and he refused to be stampeded into panic. He knew that the devil was an ace bluffer and Reinhard knew that God held the trump card.

Still, it took courage that night as he faced that small audience and still more old fashioned guts to tell his co-workers that God was going to fill the hall. The people who came were hungry for God, and this hunger kept alive Reinhard's faith. He preached and Pastor Ngidi prayed for the sick and things began to happen.

People in the audience suddenly leapt to their feet, exclaiming: "Something has happened to me. I am healed!" Others, touched by the power of God, collapsed and slumped to the floor. It was amazing and it continued night after night.

Although the team was thrilled by the miracles, they were puzzled by what to them was a new and strange phenomena: people kept falling down. Reinhard pondered the puzzle and when people began to ask what was happening this was the explanation he gave: "The Bible speaks about signs and wonders. It is not a wonder when somebody collapses, but surely it is a sign. A sign of God's presence."

And truly it was the presence of God. Reinhard had experienced little snatches of the Almighty's power in the past, but now he knew this was something bigger and better.

By the end of the first week the 800-seater city hall was packed with close to 2 000 people. They sat on top of each other, on the floor, hanging from windows. A sardine can would have looked like a palatial ballroom compared to that hall. The people were drawn in by the talk of miracles and healings. It was like the days of Jesus when the news of miracles and healings had spread across the sunny fields of Galilee and now, over 1900 years later, Jesus the Miracle Man, was walking through the city of Gaborone and the people were flocking to meet Him.

The hall was so jammed with people that it was impossible for Reinhard to get down from the platform and pray for the people. There was only one place left to go — the national sports stadium! and fortunately, that had been hired by the doubting local pastor, who by now was a transformed man and had the potential to have the biggest church in town!

It was almost like a dream when Reinhard first entered the national sports stadium. Thousands filed in to hear the gospel and what a thrill as nightly many university students streamed out to the front when the altar call was given. As a result of the crusade 500 people were baptized in water in less than two weeks.

For Reinhard this was the fulfillment of a dream. This was the dream he had nursed since the days of his youth. Crusade evangelism. Big crowds. Mighty miracles. This was what he longed to see, but had dared not share in case people thought he was a show-off.

But before the end of the crusade there was another spiritual surprise and when it came it was like an explosion.

One night while in the sports stadium the Holy Spirit urged: "Pray for the people to receive the baptism in the Holy Spirit." So he got one of his African co-workers to give a lecture on the Holy Spirit baptism. The man did his best, but it was really a jumbled up teaching and left out, what to Reinhard was the most important point: speaking in tongues was not mentioned. Reinhard decided that he would have to get up and correct this to ensure that the people understood that they had to speak in tongues as the outward evidence of having received the baptism of the Holy Spirit. As he was about to rise to his feet he was checked by the Holy Spirit: "Just keep on sitting. Stay where you are." Although frustrated, he remained seated and waited obediently on the Lord's next move.

When the people were called up to the front, about a 1 000 came down the aisles. The moment they raised their hands it was as if a bomb had exploded in their midst. Within seconds all those standing had been flattened. They lay in a disorganised mass of flesh and they were shouting and praising God in a new language.

Reinhard stood amazed, gaping at the holy disorder . . . never before had he witnessed such a thing. He had seen many people filled with the Holy Spirit and speak in tongues, but never on a scale like this. These people knew nothing about speaking in tongues. Their instruction had been incomplete, yet here they were lying on the turf of a sports stadium shouting praises to God in other tongues.

Tears filled his eyes as the scripture from the Book of Joel surfaced in his thoughts "My Spirit on all flesh . . . My Spirit on all flesh." As he stood there under the starry night sky with a symphony of heavenly languages rising into the still air he prayed: "Let your Spirit fall on all flesh in the whole world."

When he left Gaborone he made another quality

decision before God: "Lord I have tasted honey. I will never be satisfied with syrup any more. No substitute will do. It's this or nothing." And the Lord said: "I'll be with you. Go on."

He knew now beyond any shadow of doubt that God had given him a vision for Africa. Looking at the great continent of Africa, with its size, its political complexities and its heathenism, is enough to shake the faith of any mortal man. Reinhard knew, from his past experiences in Lesotho that the challenge of Africa could only be met with the power of the Holy Spirit. Anything less will only produce failure.

The pattern for his ministry was now clear. The missionary tag would disappear and his true calling would now become acknowledged by all, that of an evangelist and not a backyard one at that. No, the call was to big-time, crusade evangelism. He had tasted the first-fruits of mass evangelism and he liked it. Crowds were to become a dominant factor in his ministry. Some may criticise him for his obsession about crowds. When a crusade starts he likes to be told at the end of the evening what the count was. His official ministry publications always feature pictures of huge crowds. In fact, you're risking your head on a plate if you show him a picture that portrays a small crowd. Some may see this as vanity, or one-upmanship, and some of his own team sometimes wonder whether he doesn't get too carried away about the crowd pictures, but his explanation is simply: "The public are not interested in pictures of a handful of people. Crowds impress. If the people don't come to our tent meetings then we had better start examining ourselves."

But don't get the wrong idea that he is only happy when preaching to multi-thousand audiences. He expects that when campaigning in the tent or in stadiums in Africa, but he is at heart a humble man, who is just as much at home in a small country church. Besides the big crusades he is continually being invited by different churches to preach. He also speaks at breakfast sessions and is just at home when sharing a Bible study with his team as he is when preaching to 50 000 people

# CHAPTER NINE

## Soweto — the poor man

At the time of the exciting breakthrough into mass evangelism in Botswana another ambitious plan was being unfolded. Reinhard has a great capacity for work and it's no secret that he is more than prepared to burn himself out for Jesus. So while he was gathering together a team for Gaborone he was also initiating an unusual outreach into the African township of Soweto, which sprawls along the outskirts of Johannesburg.

The Lord had spoken to him about Soweto shortly after he had been dramatically healed in his study. The word he got from the Lord was very clear: "Soweto is like the poor man Lazarus at the door of the rich man, Johannesburg. You dare not ignore him. You've got to do something for him."

Soweto, of course, is a name that is known in many parts of the world today, mainly because of the riots and often poor social conditions which exist there. Little did Reinhard realise at the time that Soweto would make world headlines again — 18 months after he had received his charge to take the gospel to the township.

Soweto at that time, 1975, had no electricity. The streets were dust and stone, or mud and slush when it rained. Huge craters pit-marked the roads that snaked in between the dingy, grey buildings, making it a depressing place. Over 1,5-million people live there. Houses are overcrowded as family members leave their rural kraals and come to the City of Gold, Johannesburg, to find work and improve their living standards. Often as many as 15 people cram into the one-bedroom block houses, sleeping in the lounge, dining room and kitchen.

Because of high unemployment, crime is rife and shebeens, or illicit booze dens, are found in every part of the huge township. Drug traders move around its myriad of back lanes and murderers, muggers and rapists stalk the streets after sundown.

Soweto is no showpiece, but it is home to hundreds of thousands of honest folk who travel into the surrounding towns to make a living. Soweto, despite its huge social problems, the crime, the still powerful influence of witchdoctors, has a heartbeat of its own and a place in God's plan of salvation and his servant was going to present the Gospel to Soweto in a new way. It seemed obvious to Reinhard that God wanted to save many thousands, because in the middle of all that mire, there were hearts crying out for God's mercy. To accomplish his goal he adapted a bicycle strategy that he had used in Lesotho. The blueprint for his bicycle evangelism plan came to him one day while relaxing in the lounge of his modest home in Maseru.

By faith he had got together a bicycle brigade of Christian workers, who were dedicated witnesses for the Lord. He had loaded them up with Bibles, hymn books and other Christian literature and they had gone out into the lonely mountain villages selling their goods and giving their testimonies. Some of his recruits even took to horseback in order to reach some of the remote villages which nestle high up in between the rugged mountain range of the Malutis. The salesmen had worked on a commission basis and although the money was small, it provided some income for the Christians in a land where work is hard to come by.

Reinhard had hung up a huge map in his office on which were marked all the remote villages and he was thrilled as his "salesmen" reported in telling of precious souls coming to the Lord. That experience was to be put to good use as he accepted the challenge to reach Soweto. Urged on by the Holy Spirit, Reinhard followed the divine instructions explicitly. God instructed him to buy 100 bicycles, each fitted with a large box carrier on the front and the gospel witnesses were to go from house to house, street by street, giving people the Word of God in literature form, by personal testimony and also by praying for the sick.

It was an exciting commission. For a while he told no one about the vision for Soweto, except his wife. Reinhard hugged inside of his spirit that warm assurance that things would soon begin to happen. It was now a matter of being patient and waiting for God to touch the hearts of people who would become part of the Soweto outreach.

He didn't have to wait long. People began calling him on the telephone or stopping in at his office, some of them complete strangers, but all asked the same question: "Do you need a bicycle for the mission work?" Soon he had collected enough money to buy 15 of the special bicycles.

He was greatly encouraged and was struck at the

time just how quickly everything was coming together and he remarked to his wife: "It seems as though God is pushing us from behind. He is pushing us as if He were in a hurry." And there was an urgency in the task the Lord had given him, but he had no idea then what it was all about.

Realising that it was urgent to get all 100 bicycles as soon as possible Reinhard shared his vision for reaching Soweto in a church in one of the richer suburbs of Johannesburg. Financial appeals have never been a strong point in his ministry. In fact, he often sells himself short, according to some of his contemporaries, but he is very wary of coming over too strongly with appeals for money. His approach has always been to let God's people see the vision and then challenge them to become partners and share in the ministry by praying and by giving whatever they feel they can afford. Reinhard's fundamental belief is and has always been: God is the provider.

Because he is a man of high integrity, he refuses to fall into the trap of "manipulating" audiences to give money to his work. He has always believed in God's supernatural support of his ministry and he will continue to do so until Jesus returns to earth.

In 1975 he was ultra cautious about appeals for funds, and so he was thrilled after the Johannesburg church meeting when a man came up to him and without much fuss asked: "How much money do you still need for your project? How many more bicycles do you need?" Bubbling with joy Reinhard told the man he required another 85 bicycles and at R100 each he would need R8 500. "I'll give you the money for all the bicycles," promised the man.

Reinhard recalls that he was shouting hallelujahs all

the way home. In eager anticipation he visited the cycle factory and negotiated a good price and signed the contract. When he walked out of the factory and got into his parked car he had a song in his heart, but a telephone call just after he arrived home turned the lightness in his heart into a numbing deadness.

He decided to phone the willing sponsor and give him the details of the contract price that he had been able to negotiate. As he spoke the man's voice interrupted him: "I have made a mistake. I am sorry. I cannot give you anything." Holding the receiver to his ear Reinhard wondered whether his ears were playing a trick on him or whether the would-be sponsor was just a joker. But the man was deadly serious and Reinhard was left holding a signed and sealed contract for 85 bicycles and not a cent with which to pay for them when they were delivered. His free-wheeling spirit of joy braked to an abrupt halt.

In this incident Reinhard portrayed his usual steely calm and determination and his total reliance upon God. While some men may have been quick to tear a strip off the errant bicycle sponsor and try to bully him into keeping his promise, he allowed him to withdraw his offer and made a gesture which marks his humility before God. "I told him I wanted to remain friends and if he couldn't trust God, then he should trust me to trust God!" It is a trait of his not to make enemies and to the best of his ability never to bear grudges.

So ensuring that he retained his cool and his sanctification Reinhard now sat down to face the problem and he wasn't helped by some so-called friends. Some of them were obviously close relatives of Job's comforter's because when they heard of the misfortune over the bicycle money they began to criticise and doubt his vision for Soweto. For the next few days he faced comments like: "We always knew it was a mistake." "This was too big a bite. We knew you were going to choke to death." One asked:"Why 100 bikes. Is that a magical figure?" To which Bonnke gave the cutting reply: "No, it's not. It's God's figure and that is all there is to it."

That type of criticism only goaded him on and he realised one of his many favourite slogans which he sprinkles liberally into his sermons, "When the going gets tough, the tough get going". And he did. Refusing to be swayed by the critics or the doubters he continued to plan the forthcoming Soweto outreach and within the next four weeks the finance flowed into the ministry. He had continued to share the Soweto vision and Christians were touched and rallied to support him. Not only was the R8 500 supplied for the bicycles, but an additional R22 000 swelled the bank balance, thanks to the generosity of the German Christians, who became the main contributors when Reinhard visited his homeland for a brief preaching tour and told them of the bicycle project.

So with military-like planning Operation Soweto was mounted. A huge map dominated the ministry offices and with 100 trained Christian workers the bicycle brigade set out to carry the gospel into every corner of the vast suburb of Soweto. Of great help in accomplishing this massive job was Pastor Johan Venter, of the AFM. He was a key figure in the organizing and running of this exciting new way of reaching the people of Soweto. The bicycle evangelists did a tremendous job, working long hours each day and within eight months the target had been reached.

And then it happened. The last evangelist had hardly pedalled back into the depot when Reinhard received the news: "Soweto is aflame." That was June 1976. Large scale rioting had broken out. The police had been called in. The army was on standby and cars and buses were being stoned and burned. Lawlessness reigned for several weeks and thousands of workers stayed home, afraid to venture onto the streets which had become the scene of vicious fighting as rioters clashed head-on with police. Many died. At night the sky towards the south-west of Johannesburg was a red glow as the burning and pillaging continued.

Now Reinhard knew why God had been in such a hurry and why 100 bicycles had been needed. Less than that number and they would never have completed the project in time. In fact, it was so uncanny that many people came to him afterwards and said: "Did you know beforehand that the riots were on the cards?" Looking back he admits that the Soweto episode made a lasting impression on his commitment and walk with the Lord. "What if I had not obeyed? What if I had compromised on the number of bicycles? I determined more than ever to walk a strict path of obedience, never questioning God's wisdom."

Another lesson he learnt was that God never has to rely on just one man to finance His projects. Although initially disappointed when the man withdrew his offer to pay for the bicycles, Reinhard received one of those gracious "pick-me-ups" from the Lord when an elderly lady visited him the day after his big let down. The woman gave him enough money to buy one bicycle and told him: "Every day I will think of that man on my bicycle going from door to door. I will be praying for that man every day." It was then that he realised that God not only wanted bicycles and evangelists, but he wanted a prayer partner to back up each one of the men out in the field. Gold and silver were not the things that impressed God. No, He wanted people to pray for His work.

And the bicycle evangelists needed prayer support because Soweto was a tough place and it took real courage to take the Word of God from house to house and to give a personal testimony.

One of the evangelists had this fascinating story to tell after a hot day on the dusty streets. He stopped at a house and went inside. The only person he could see was a small boy. He asked if there were any adults at home. The child told him that his brother was in the next room so the worker went through and found a young man lying on a bed, the covers pulled over his head. The worker wanted to know why he was hiding in bed in the middle of the day.

A conversation was started and the bicycle evangelist began to explain the Good News to him. Suddenly the young man leapt out of the bed and exclaimed: "I have killed someone. The police are hunting for me." The evangelist pressed on and the young man broke down in tears and together they knelt on the bare floor in prayer. A sudden banging came to the door and a group of policemen barged in. They stopped at the bedroom door to witness the killer giving his heart to the Lord. They stood back and waited and when the young man rose to his feet they handcuffed him. In his prayer of repentance the man had confessed to committing a murder and the police had heard it.

This was just one of a thousand incidents, of how the Holy Spirit worked to bring Jesus Christ into the lives of countless homes in Soweto.

But Reinhard was not finished with Soweto. He would return, not once, but twice and the second time would herald the launching of the world's biggest gospel tent. But that vision was still hidden from view.

# CHAPTER TEN

## Nursing for Jesus

Reinhard shifted smoothly into the role of a crusade evangelist. He never missed a beat as he cast aside the traditional missionary style and confidently donned the mantle of the big-time, travelling evangelist. He's never been short of confidence and took every new challenge in his stride. His confidence is infectious because it is not tinged with any pride, in fact, it is one of the secrets of his success as a preacher. He communicates this confidence and because of his absolute devotion to the Lord, the Holy Spirit's anointing is always apparent in his meetings. But with all his confidence he is humble — but not shy and his boyish cheek gets him favours that others would never dare to ever ask for — even if they had an angel standing next to them.

In 1976 he was already into the crusade pattern. After the breakthrough in Gaborone in early 1975 he had followed up with further crusades, including a highly successful one in Cape Town in November-December. It was at this crusade that he turned photographer to capture a miracle on film. After delivering his message and giving the altar call he had handed over the meeting to Pastor Ngidi, who began to pray for the sick. Among the large audience were several people in wheelchairs, who waited patiently among the long line of people. Led by the Holy Spirit, Reinhard grabbed his camera and took a picture of just one of the wheelchair victims — a woman, who was still waiting for Pastor Ngidi to get to her and pray. When the barrel-chested Pastor Ngidi came to the woman he prayed simply: "In the name of Jesus, stand up." The power of God shot through her lame joints and she stood up jubilantly waving her arms as the audience broke into spontaneous praise and quickly giving his camera to a colleague, Reinhard posed in the "after" picture with Pastor Ngidi, an empty wheelchair and a smiling ex-cripple.

The pace got even hotter on the crusade trail the next year. Besides the on-going Soweto project, three other high points of 1976 were the Port Elizabeth crusade, one in Windhoek, in South West Africa, or as it is more commonly known today, Namibia, and the closing one of the year in Swaziland.

Early in 1976 the property on which the present Christ For All Nations headquarters stands, was purchased. Like everything connected with this extraordinary ministry it is an event worth recording.

He had been looking for a suitable piece of land, preferably near to where he stayed. One day a Mr Rogers, who lived in the Witfield area, approached him and told him about a certain property.

"There's a Scotsman living in the old white house on the plot near to the railway line and he wants to sell it to me to use as a nursery school, but I'm not too keen on it. Would you like to have a look?" asked Mr Rogers.

Quick to sense a divine opportunity Reinhard hopped into his car and sped up the road to view the property. It was a bumpy, dusty track they drove along and when they arrived it didn't look very impressive. There was an old farmhouse on the property – it used to be white, but it had turned a sickly yellow with age and it was surrounded by tall grass and a glorious crop of weeds. It was no Garden of Eden. But right from the moment the soles of his feet touched that property he "knew" it would be his headquarters. He immediately got down to the task of buying the property – not an easy task because he had no funds available.

A friend of his, Clive Hopkins, from Britain, who worked as editor of his ministry publication Revival Report for a time, started the legal negotiations with the municipal authorities. After one visit to the municipality Hopkins returned looking rather despondent and as he sat in Reinhard's office he rattled off ten reasons why the authorities would squash the deal – even if they had the money to buy the ground. Hopkins was flumoxed by the reply he received: "The reasons are in our favour" and Hopkins left the office shaking his head. No bureaucratic red tape, or any municipal official was going to stand in the way. The land would be his. The price in the meantime had been agreed upon, and after discussing the matter with the CFAN Board members he convinced them to go ahead and close the deal. He confidently told them at the meeting: "In the name of Jesus I will pay the full amount on the day of transfer." Three months later he sat down at his desk, and with a flourish of a pen wrote out a cheque for the full amount. The Lord had provided a blessed cash flow into the ministry that would have made him the envy of the best businessmen in Johannesburg.

His Board members were a bit perplexed when they

saw the land, though. Standing waist-high in the overgrown grass, one of his Board members quipped: "Maybe Reinhard is going farming." He wondered himself.

Early in 1976 Reinhard and his evangelistic team campaigned in New Brighton, Port Elizabeth, where a powerful move of the Holy Spirit brought such strong conviction that people openly renounced their past by voluntarily turning over stolen goods and throwing away witchcraft fetishes and in some cases murderous weapons.

The Centenary Hall, which seated 4 000 people, was hired for the two-week crusade and on one Tuesday evening the power of God moved so mightily that Reinhard failed to finish his sermon. All of a sudden people started streaming to the front, weeping like children. A packet of cigarettes suddenly landed on the platform, thrown by somebody among the sobbing crowd. It was quickly followed by a shower of more tobacco, knives and other murderous instruments, witchcraft fetishes and stolen articles.

"I'll always remember one woman who came forward for salvation at that meeting. Weeping and in obvious distress, she came up to the platform and pulled off a beautiful white jersey she was wearing and threw it at my feet. At first I did not understand what was happening. In fact, I was a little concerned when I saw her take off the jersey. You never know what some people do when they are simply emotionally stirred up. I leaned over to the woman and asked her what was wrong. With tears streaming down her cheeks she sobbed out: 'Stolen.' She could no longer bear to have the jersey anywhere near her." It was a truly glorious breakthrough for the gospel and the word soon spread through New Brighton that things were happening in the big hall. At the close of the campaign close to 2 000 people had made decisions for Jesus.

One night a young man pushed his way up the aisle. As he came toward the platform Reinhard spotted something in his hand. It was a vicious looking knife, probably homemade, but it looked heavy enough to cut the throat of an elephant! He was a young man, probably about 20 years old, but his face was a network of scars — trademarks of the many knife fights he had been involved in. As their eyes met, the young man spoke: "Here, pastor, take it." He pushed the knife into Reinhard's hand. "I have decided to give my heart to Jesus." Flooded by a wave of compassion Reinhard leaned over and put his arm around the young man, hugging him and whispering:"Thank you Lord. What no policemen could ever do has just been done now by the Holy Spirit." This was what the famous English preacher Charles Haddon Spurgeon meant when he once wrote "I don't want a church in the vale . . . give me a mission at the gates of hell!". Yes, the CFAN team were plucking precious lives out of the very presence of hell.

From, the seaside city of Port Elizabeth the CFAN crusade team headed north-west, across the desert to Windhoek where they held a crusade in the township of Katutura during June and July. With him on this crusade was his usual co-evangelist Pastor Ngidi, who was again mightily used by God while praying for the sick. However, Ngidi could only spend a week in Windhoek and a young pastor, Michael Kolisang, took over the ministry of praying for the sick after the gospel services. Kolisang was one of the most devoted members of the CFAN team – and still is. His association with Bonnke goes back to the first days in Maseru, Lesotho.

Kolisang, a young, zealous supporter of a local political party in Lesotho, had been a spectator at the big bus depot in Maseru when the sound of a piano accordion caught his attention. He wandered over to an open space where he saw a White man playing the music and singing religious songs. Curiosity caused him to linger and as a small crowd gathered the man laid down his accordion and with a Bible waving in one hand began to preach about Jesus. At the end of the service Kolisang was deeply distressed by what he heard. He wanted to get right with God and he wanted to know more about Jesus. Kolisang waited for the crowd to disperse and then went to speak to Reinhard. The way of salvation was explained to him and it was in a VW Kombi, parked at the Maseru bus depot, that Kolisang gave his heart to the Lord.

Kolisang was soon aware that God had chosen him for the ministry and turned his back on a potentially fruitful political career to follow Jesus. Through Reinhard he was given a Bible school training and soon he was out holding his own meetings. The pair often joined forces and although it seemed for a while that they were to be permanently separated when Reinhard left Lesotho, Kolisang later followed him to South Africa. Despite being a fulltime member of the team, he was very much in the shadow of the more senior Pastor Ngidi, and had to wait patiently for his opportunities. His faithfulness to the CFAN ministry has been richly rewarded and today he is a key figure in the plan to win Africa for Jesus.

While in Windhoek Reinhard had the opportunity

to pray for a deaf man and see for himself a wonderful, creative miracle. He was staying with a local minister, Pastor Van Wyk, and late one morning a man came knocking at the door. The man, a Mr Smit, had just been released from hospital and hearing that Pastor Bonnke was in town, had come to the house to be prayed for. The man was suffering from cancer in one ear and had no eardrum in the other. As they stood together in the middle of the lounge Reinhard placed his hands firmly on the man's ears and, looking him straight in the eyes asked: "Do you believe that Jesus is going to heal you?" And as the man gave an affirmative reply he began to pray: "O, God I'm asking for two things: heal that cancerous ear and perform a miracle in the other ear." When he had finished praying he asked the man to close the ear he could hear with and suddenly the man started to jump in the air — he could hear with the ear that had no eardrum! Incredulously Reinhard looked on and admits that as he watched he began to doubt what he was seeing: "How can a man hear with an ear that has no eardrum? Then suddenly it struck me . . . God who created you and me in the first instance, surely He must have all the spare parts that we would ever need!"

That sums up much of his approach to healing. Although many theologians debate the pros and cons of healing and many Christians squabble about reasons why people do not receive healing, Reinhard sails along praying for the sick. If they get healed he rejoices with them and praises God, if they don't he calmly rests the case in the care of God's sovereign will and great mercy. Once, while praying he admits that he pondered the controversy surrounding divine healing and put some questions before the Lord. It was from the insight God gave him on this occasion that he formulated his attitude toward praying for the sick.

The Lord showed him that he was the "nurse" — Jesus was the Great Physician. As he pondered this seemingly amusing analogy he began to see the depth of truth in it. "The more I thought about it, the happier I became. I suddenly realised that it is the duty of the doctor to diagnose the disease, and it is the duty of the doctor to prescribe the medicine and all that I have to do is follow behind the doctor and carry the medicine. It just remains for me to administer it the way it is prescribed - and then it works. The medicine is red in colour '. . . by His stripes we are healed', the prescription says '. . . and they shall lay hands on the sick and the sick shall recover.' So all I am is a nurse — and I'm very happy to be one for Jesus."

Certainly not a thesis with which to win a professorship, and some may scoff at its naive simplicity but when it comes to preaching the gospel Reinhard believes in simplicity. Many preachers come to listen to him because they want to observe his style, his presentation and to hear the message. His delivery is certainly powerful, typical of the stoked-up evangelist, pitching his voice at various levels to paint a landscape of words for his audience. On the platform he is regal — like a lion proudly guarding his domain he demands the attention of every eye. As he develops his sermon he becomes for a moment in time John the Baptist, rugged and raw as he condemns sin and points people to Jesus. Then deftly the mood changes and he is a young David soothing the agitated King Saul. Tender words of love tug at heart strings as he continues to uplift Jesus and then with a final swirl the gospel net is thrown out and like Peter on the shores of Galilee, he pulls in the straining net as hundreds respond to the altar call. And after gently and triumphantly leading them in a prayer of repentance he becomes the "nurse", as the sick, lame and blind stream forward.

During 1976 he witnessed two other remarkable healings, both involving people who were suffering from terminal cancer. The one involved a married woman, Mrs Dinnie Viljoen of Pretoria. She had been widowed and had remarried and in July 1974, four months after her marriage, she had taken ill. She was operated on and the verdict was a deadly cancer, that would gradually spread through her body and kill her. She went through 18 months of treatment, in and out of hospital all the time, but she was a dying woman. All that she had left was her faith in God. While in hospital her husband bought her a booklet to read. It was all about a passage of scripture found in Habakkuk 3:19 "The Lord God is my strength and He has made my feet like those of a deer, and makes me walk on high places." Mrs Viljoen believed this scripture held some significant meaning for her and in her daily devotions recalled it to mind time and again.

During one of her frequent stays in hospital a Christian nurse gave her a cassette of a sermon by Reinhard Bonnke. Later Mrs Viljoen recalled the occasion: "As I listened to the tape faith rose up in my heart as I heard of the miracles God performed through the ministry of Pastor Bonnke and his co-worker, Pastor Kolisang. In my extreme weakness I murmured a prayer: 'Lord Jesus, if it is Your will that my path should cross with this Pastor Bonnke and his colleague so that they can pray for me, then help me please Lord.' Later I told my husband about the wonderful message I had listened to, but said nothing about my whispered plea to God.

"I was finally sent home from hospital, very weak and full of pain. A week later an old acquaintance phoned and told me that God had revealed to him that he must bring a certain Pastor Bonnke to pray for my healing that very day. I was overwhelmed with joy and thankfulness."

When Reinhard received the telephone call from Mrs Viljoen's friend his first reaction was to say he was too busy and could not make a special trip to Pretoria. (He was engaged in a conference at the time). But he felt the checking of the Holy Spirit and the words materialised in his heart: "I am sending you," the Lord said.

"All right," he told the man on the other end of the telephone, "I'll come, on condition that you come with me and show me the way to the woman's house." He agreed and they arranged to meet in Kempton Park, which was about 10 minutes drive from the Bonnke's home. As it turned out Michael Kolisang had arrived only that morning from Lesotho and so he went along for the ride with Reinhard. When they met their guide he gave a slightly perplexed glance at Kolisang and said: "Look, I have nothing against Black people, pastor, he's a dear brother, but we are going to Dutch Reformed people. The dying woman is Dutch Reformed and I don't think they would like a Black man to come into the house."

Reinhard replied: "Don't worry, Mike understands South Africa. He can wait in the car while I pray for the woman in her house."

As they drove along the Johannesburg-Pretoria highway the racial question, roused by the presence of his colleague Michael, soon faded from his mind. Silently he prayed about the woman he was going to visit. Clearly the Lord was in the matter, but what must he tell her and which scripture could he give, he thought? Then suddenly verses from the Old Testament flashed into his mind, from the book of Habakkuk 3:17,18: "Although the fig tree shall not blossom, neither shall fruit be in the vines; the labour of the olive shall fail, and the fields shall yield no meat; the flock shall be cut off from the fold, and there shall be no herd in the stalls: Yet I will rejoice in the Lord, I will joy in the God of my salvation."

As they neared the outskirts of Pretoria Reinhard wrestled with the scripture: "But Lord, I can't give her that scripture. It sounds as though she is going to die. I mean . . . 'the fig tree won't blossom, no herd in the stall . . . everything goes wrong . . . ' No Lord! But the Holy Spirit clearly indicated once again: ' Give her that scripture. '

As they drew up in front of the Viljoen home, Reinhard leaned over to Kolisang and asked him: "Please wait here while we go inside and pray for this lady." As he went through the front gate he still felt uncomfortable about the scripture the Lord had given him, but he was determined now to discharge his mission as commanded. They were let into the house by a servant and led down a passage and into a bedroom. Propped up among a bunch of pillows lay Mrs Viljoen. Death was written across her face.

At first she didn't realise that she had visitors. Then her dark, sunken eyes flickered alive and from her thin, pale lips she exclaimed: "Pastor Bonnke! You came to visit me. This is a wonderful answer to prayer." The mask of death seemed to lift from her face. The lifeless face that had been framed by the pillows was suddenly animated as she told him about the cassette of his that she had listened to in hospital and about her weakly murmured prayer that she might meet up with Reinhard and Kolisang.

At the mention of Kolisang's name, Reinhard exclaimed: "Just a minute my sister I'll call Kolisang — he's right here with me now. He's waiting in the car outside!"

With great haste Kolisang was beckoned in and it was obvious to Reinhard that there was no racial prejudice, as he and Kolisang stood at Mrs Viljoen's bedside. As they stood there Reinhard opened his Bible to the book of Habakkuk and read the scripture that he felt prompted to share at that moment with Mrs Viljoen: "The fig tree shall not blossom, there is no food in the field, no herd in the stall, yet I will rejoice in the Lord my God. He will make my feet to be like hinds' feet." As he read, Mrs Viljoen began to weep.

"Please stop," she said in between sobs, "I must tell you what happened. While I was lying in hospital I asked my husband to get me a certain book by Andrew Murray on prayer. They didn't have the book so it was ordered. Later the bookshop telephoned my husband to tell him the book had arrived and he went in to fetch it. However, my husband wasn't quite sure which title I wanted and he took the wrong book. It was called "Hinds Feet on High Places." The whole book is just on that scripture. Here it is."

Her frail hand pushed a book toward Reinhard and as he took it and opened it he saw that almost every sentence had been underlined."Well, I am convinced that God is here to do a miracle," he told her and the little group gathered around the bed and as they laid hands on Mrs Viljoen the room was filled with the glory of God. Mrs Viljoen whispered: "I have a vision . . . I see myself standing under a mighty waterfall.''

When they finished praying Mrs Viljoen was already looking stronger. She had been wonderfully healed in an instant. As Reinhard and Kolisang left the bedroom to rush back to attend the Johannesburg conference they couldn't help but notice the contrast. Only a half an hour earlier death had stalked that home. Now life, the abundant life that Jesus promised pulsated through the woman and the very walls and doors of the home seemed to vibrate with life.

Five days after being prayed for Mrs Viljoen was scheduled for another visit to the hospital for further tests. At the time Mrs Viljoen wondered whether she should cancel the visit, but she felt convinced that she should go ahead and allow the tests to be done. Then followed three days of intensive tests at the Cancer Research Institute and after all the X-rays and everything had been completed the tests proved negative. The doctors and her specialist were astonished — there was not a trace of cancer to be found.

The sequel to this remarkable healing was felt in many parts of the country because God not only healed Mrs Viljoen, but gave her a ministry to the Afrikaans-speaking people of her church. She criss-crossed the nation for a year, telling her story and seeing countless women won to the Lord and set free from religious bondage.

One day Reinhard received a telephone call from Mrs Viljoen. ''Pastor Bonnke it's the anniversary of my healing and I'm having a thanksgiving service at my home. I've invited about 40 women to attend. Will you be the speaker?'' He gladly accepted. Half an hour later the phone rang again. It was Mrs Viljoen again. "Sorry to bother you again, but the 40 has become 400. I've got permission to use the Presbyterian church down the road. Will you still come?" "Yes, of course," he told her.

It was a wonderful thanksgiving service as the Holy Spirit ministered to those women in a very special way. Mrs Viljoen was full of joy and her love for the Lord just overflowed. She was radiantly happy as he waved goodbye and drove off on that afternoon. It was the last time he was to see Mrs Viljoen.

The next day he flew to West Germany on a preaching tour and while away she died. In fact, he returned home on the day of her funeral. Remembering the incident he still firmly believes that if he had been in South Africa at the time and been able to pray with and counsel her she would not have died. "Of course, I can only speculate about that, but I do know that God had extended her life for one wonderful year. And during those 12 months she accomplished more for the Lord than she had done in all her previous years."

Later, in the same year of 1976, he was again called upon to pray for a terminally ill person. He was asked to visit a Mr Kruger who was in the cancer ward of the Johannesburg General Hospital.

Leaving home with his wife one afternoon they drove to the hospital and were unable to find any parking, so hopping out at the entrance gates he told his wife to "keep orbiting while I go and pray for this man."

As he entered the hospital the familiar antiseptic smell caught his nostrils as he pushed his way through the visitors blocking the passage. He found the ward, a general ward with 20 odd beds in it. He paused at the doorway to ask a passing sister to direct him to Mr Kruger's bed. His footsteps echoed on the shiny linoleum flooring as he drew near to the iron bed with its typical white cover over a still form lying on the bed. As he drew alongside the bed he looked at an ashen-faced man, his chest heaving as he seemed to battle for each breath. He was a man of about Bonnke's own age and as he recalls the "handwriting of death was all over his face".

When Mr Kruger saw Reinhard he urged him to bend over so he could speak. " Pastor Bonnke. . ." he gasped, '. . .have you got a word from God for me?" As he looked into those dark, pleading eyes, the Spirit of God moved in Reinhard's heart.

"Yes," he replied, "I've got a word from God for you. You shall not die, but live and declare the works of the Lord." (Psalm 118:17). The straining head collapsed back onto the pillow and Reinhard sat for a while reading the Word of God to him and then praying for him.

He seemed to relax when Reinhard placed his hand on his arm and as he left Mr Kruger managed a weak smile as he said: "Oh, thank you Lord." Mr Kruger was suffering from leukemia as were most of the others in the ward. It was a ward of death — not many men ever walked out alive once they had been committed to this ward. Leaving Mr Kruger, Reinhard hurried down the corridors to find his wife patiently circling the hospital, still unable to find a parking space.

He never heard anything more about Mr Kruger until a year later. One day while sitting at his desk in his office at the CFAN headquarters a knock came to the door and in strode a strapping young man. He really looked hail and hearty and as Reinhard rose to greet him, he put out his hand and said: "Pastor Bonnke, do you remember me?"

That, of course is always an embarrassing question for a travelling evangelist who sees and prays for thousands of people each year. He studied the face for a few moments, then had to confess he couldn't place the man at all.

The man sat down and then, with tears in his eyes, he said: "I'm Kruger, the man from that cancer ward you visited in Johannesburg." Reinhard stared across his desk in amazement, followed shortly by a hearty "hallelujah!" This was his story:

"Well, pastor, all those other men from that ward are dead and buried. I came here to tell you my story.

"When you left that ward that afternoon I knew the power of God had struck at the cause of my disease. I called a nurse and told her to get my clothes. I told her: 'I'm going home. Jesus has healed me.' The nurse wasn't impressed. She thought I was losing my senses. But I insisted. 'Call the doctors. I'm leaving. Please get my clothes,' I told the nurse.

"The doctors came. They didn't want to let me out, but I stubbornly insisted. They said it was impossible. I said it was possible. After a while they agreed, on condition that I sign a document that absolved them of any responsibility should I die on the way out or at home. I agreed because I knew I was not going to die.

"I left the ward, carrying a medicine chest. The doctors gave me 400 cortisone tablets. I was to take 40 of them a day. That would keep me going for 10 days, they said. I really didn't want to take them, but to satisfy everybody I took them and staggered out of the hospital.

"Back home I threw all the tablets in the dustbin. And I began to get better and regained my strength. God had healed me. I was going to live. I went back to the hospital and the doctors were amazed at my improvement. They examined me thoroughly, but could find no trace of leukemia. When I looked in at my old ward all the other patients were gone . . . buried.

"Yes, I am perfectly well. I don't even suffer from the slightest headache. There is no sign that I was in the jaws of death. I am a picture of health, thanks to Jesus," concluded Mr Kruger.

Reinhard Bonnke the "nurse" rejoiced heartily with Mr Kruger and his story featured prominently in the CFAN ministry magazine, Revival Report. Mr Kruger is still well and lives at Springs, on the East Rand.

# CHAPTER 11

## Plan like a millionaire

The final big crusade of 1976 was held in Swaziland. It was held at two venues — Manzini and in Mbabane. It had several highlights. One was the tremendous demonic opposition, the other was an opportunity to hold a special meeting for the royal household of Swaziland and the third was the weather — bad weather.

Ever since he started his crusade meetings, he had been at the mercy of the weather. In Cape Town the meetings had outgrown the hall they had hired, but when they went outdoors, the bitterly cold wind kept people away. It was the same in Port Elizabeth. He had recognised that the only way to draw consistently big crowds was to provide weatherproof conditions. The answer was a tent.

All through 1976 he had made appeals for funds to get a tent, but one of substantial size, something large enough to hold at least 5 000 people, and maybe more if possible. But finance, of course, was the big hurdle.

Then at Mbabane one afternoon there was a cloud-burst. The heavens opened and it was as though the Victoria Falls was overhead. Reinhard had been using a small tent, which offered limited protection from the elements for 800 people or so, but on this particular afternoon there was no protection for anyone as the rain pelted down. The meeting place where the tiny tent had been pitched was a gently sloping, basin-like area, and torrents of water came rushing down into this low-lying ground.

As the torrents washed through the flimsy tent Reinhard watched helplessly as cripples were taken by the current and struggled and splashed as they tried to drag themselves up onto higher ground. "It broke my heart to see those sick and crippled people lie there in all that water, unable to move," he recalls and as he opened his heart to God he cried: "My God, please give us a roof over our heads." Quick as a flash the answer came back to his spirit: "Trust Me for a tent that will seat 10 000." As he looked at the swirling water, the soaked and wretched people standing in the driving rain he answered: "I trust you."

That private little prayer meeting in the middle of a thunderstorm on an open field in Swaziland would bear much fruit. God would one day give him a tent so huge, that when he stood under its immense roof he could hardly believe that men could have built such a thing. But for the time being, that was hidden from view. His immediate vision was for a tent large enough to hold 10 000 people.

When they had completed their meetings in Swaziland he returned to Johannesburg and immediately started to enquire about a tent, one that could hold 10 000 people. As he telephoned around and as he went and saw people they all doubted whether such a tent was possible. Certainly there was nobody in South Africa at that time who could make a tent that size. And when he heard the cost he felt a bit weak in the knees. One firm told him that the tent which he envisaged would cost about R100 000.

Although the CFAN ministry was growing with new staff, transport and publications, finance was restricted. The quote of R100 000 made him feel as though he had been dealing in small change up to then. Could the missionary/evangelist now become a high pressure financier? The answer was "yes". He almost amazed himself with his boldness, but if God wanted him to have such a tent, he would have to trust God for the money — even if it was six figures.

But where should he start? How should he plan? It was while he was pondering his plan that God spoke words that still ring loud and clear to this day: "Don't plan with that which is in your own pockets. Plan with that which is in My pocket."

Never slow to see the truth of revelation, Reinhard dug into his own pockets and all he felt were a few copper coins, but then he caught a vision of God's pocket. It was full! and he prayed: "Lord, if you will allow me to plan with what is in your pocket, then I will plan like a millionaire!"

Again it was the dedication, devotion and generosity of the growing number of prayer partners in Germany and South Africa who made the new tent a reality. The tent was designed and the work carried out by an Italian firm in Milan while the platform and steelwork were done locally.

When 1976 closed he had his eyes firmly fixed on getting a crusade tent in the next year. There was not only the cost of the tent to be considered. Vehicles were needed to transport the tent, a powerful generator was needed and more personnel, of course. CFAN was going to expand even further. But in the meanwhile the open air crusades continued and in January 1977 the team went to the Northern

Transvaal to hold a crusade at a place called Bushbuckridge. The popular Pastor Ngidi, who had been associated with Reinhard since the Botswana breakthrough, had been scheduled to accompany the team, but pulled out at the last minute. His responsibilities for his district in Natal were making it difficult for him to make time for the increasing number of crusades and he "retired" from CFAN.

When Pastor Ngidi failed to arrive for the Bushbuckridge crusade Reinhard felt a bit anxious because the big Zulu preacher had been used mightily when praying for the sick and he wondered how the meetings would fair without him. But a comforting "Do not be afraid . . . I will be with you" from the Lord, reassured him.

A voluntary helper, Israel Malele had gone ahead to prepare the crusade and when he arrived at the venue, a school, he found that a makeshift auditorium had been made by joining two tents together. On the first night there was a wonderful miracle when a young cripple woman, who had hobbled into the meeting on crutches, was healed. She had tossed her crutches aside and to the delight of the crowd had walked up and down the platform for all to see what Jesus had done for her. The result on the villages and district was electrifying and within two days the crowd had grown to 5 000.

Another dramatic healing further confirmed the gospel message when a 19-year-old man received his sight. Reinhard, led by the Holy Spirit asked for totally blind people to be brought forward for prayer. As they stood before him he told the 20 blind people who had been led forward by relatives and friends: "I am going to pray for you one by one. Keep your eyes closed. When I have laid hands on your eyes, continue to keep them shut. Then I will stand in front of you and I will command you in the Name of Jesus to open your eyes. When you open your eyes you are going to see a White man standing in front of you. I believe this.''

The blind people shuffled forward, some with white canes, others helped by young people. It was a pathetic scene as he moved along the line, laying hands on each of the blind people.

Then he stood in front of them and commanded their eyes to open. His voice had hardly stopped echoing through the night air when a young man let out a scream in front of him. The man leapt forward, pointing his finger and exclaiming: ''There you are. I can see you.'' The crowd burst into spontaneous praise. People hugged one another. Others collapsed under the power of God. It was a real glory meeting!

Another remarkable incident happened in the same series of meetings. An African woman, highly educated, came up to Reinhard after a meeting and told him her story: ''Because I was deaf I sat in the front row and read your lips. You preached on forgiveness. My husband treated me so badly that I could not forgive him. But as you preached I was touched in my heart and I prayed, 'Lord, I forgive my husband', and at that very moment my ears popped open.''

Although it is the spectacular healings and miracles that draw the crowd — as it did in the days of Jesus — Reinhard never questions God why some get healed and some do not. Over the years he has learned to trust God and in the middle of all the thrilling miracles at Bushbuckridge the Lord inserted a poignant vision which deeply impressed him.

One evening he was moving past a line of people praying for them when he stopped in front of an elderly woman, who had no eyes in her eye sockets. He prayed for her and moved on. While praying for the next person he heard the blind woman weeping and then whispering quietly : "I see, I see, I see." He turned immediately to look into her face and asked her:

"Tell me what do you see? Can you see me? She replied: "No. I cannot see you. But I see a white cross and I see Jesus there."

He stood anchored to the ground for a few moments, looking into those eye sockets that had no vision and silently pondered the "miracle". "Is it possible Lord that eyeless eyes see more than the finest physical eyes? Somebody with only eye sockets can see Jesus, and those that have the sharpest eagle eyes often cannot see Him at all." God took that woman's blindness away in a different manner and today she is a dear child of God.

During this crusade his host was a local man Mr Stick Nyalungu, an elderly businessman who ran his own transport business. He also had five wives, which, of course, is permitted by African custom. (He became a Christian after his marriages). The man was getting on in years and he had a bad limp and was finding it increasingly more difficult to get around without aid.

One day he asked Reinhard to pray for him and as he did so there was a flash of heaven's power and the man's lame leg pulsed with life again. He jumped up and down on the previously bad leg and shouted: "Look at me. I can kick the dog again!"

After he had calmed down, he sent one of his buses to round up all his relatives in the district to bring them to his home for a service and to tell them about his healing. It was a mini crusade and Mr Nyalungu had the joy of seeing many of his relatives brought to the Lord.

One night as Reinhard drove up to his host's home, he noticed a police van parked nearby. Mr Nyalungu met him outside the door and whispered that the police were waiting for him. At first he thought he had done something wrong and had unwittingly broken some regulations and so he told his host to ask the policemen in. As they entered the room, instead of the expected air of authority, a uniformed policeman bowed humbly and said: "Pastor, we have heard about the miracles of God. Will you pray for us?" Reinhard smiled to himself — the strong arm of the law was humbled as God saved with a mighty arm of salvation.

# CHAPTER 12

## A heap of crutches

Bushbuckridge got 1977 off to a thrilling start, but greater things were still to come. The building on the present office complex at Witfield was started and the order for the gospel tent was made and due for arrival for use at the start of 1978. On the crusade scene the CFAN team, now acquiring more vehicles, and caravans, were learning more and more that being a member of a travelling evangelistic band was not a glamorous affair. Some of the major crusades of the year were at Giyani, in Gazankulu, Sibasa in Vendaland, Phalaborwa, Tzaneen, Messina and Louis Trichard. Of these, two merit special attention – the April crusade at Giyani and the one in August at Sibasa, the capital of Vendaland.

Giyani is a remote rural area, tucked up in the north east, bordering Vendaland and Mozambique. The nearest town of any size is Tzaneen, about 150 km to the south. The venue for the meetings was a school hall. The only publicity given to the meetings were the distribution of handbills. But the team need not have worried about pre-publicity for the meetings because what happened was the best advertising you could get in the whole universe – and it didn't cost a cent.

On the first night about 100 people arrived. The

next night there were 300 people. On both nights people got saved and people got healed and it was the physical miracles that attracted the crowds. The local people may not have recognized their desperate spiritual needs, but they knew that they had need of physical healing and by the third night the tiny school hall was a crush of flesh as over a thousand people crammed into a hall designed to hold 400 people. They overflowed outside and sat perched in open windows to hear the gospel and to see the miracles.

The team were thrilled with the fantastic response, especially in such a remote area. But with it came a problem. The headmaster of the school came to see Reinhard on the morning of the fourth day. Although he was not against having the meetings in his school hall he pointed out that it was designed to hold only 400 people and that with such a huge crowd descending things were, to put it politely, becoming unhygienic . . .

Where could they go? The schoolmaster suggested the local agricultural showgrounds at the town eight kilometres away. Reinhard wasn't happy about changing the venue, not with such a wonderful response after only three nights. Would these people travel the extra distance to come to the meetings if they were moved to the showgrounds? Many were already walking long distances to get to the school.

However, there was no alternative and so they switched to the showgrounds, but true to tradition the people of Gazankulu continued to attend. The meetings at the school had created excitement throughout the whole area and up to 8 000 people crammed in to the showgrounds for the remaining nights of the crusade. Blind eyes were opened and cripples walked. In fact, one of the most amazing crusade photographs ever taken was captured during the Giyani outreach because at the end of the crusade they had a mountain of crutches and walking sticks that cripples had thrown aside after being healed. Wherever the CFAN team drove people came out along the side of the road to wave and demonstrate the joy of their salvation. The whole area was alive with new life.

One day Reinhard popped into the local post office and as he approached the counter the young attendant behind it gaped at him with wide eyes. "Pastor Bonnke!" he exclaimed. "Yes," he replied. Tears filled the teller's eyes as he spoke again: "Umfundis (a local term for pastor or teacher) I must tell you something. I was a heathen, a real heathen. I never set foot inside a church. I had nothing to do with Christianity. I was a drunkard. I tormented my wife. Then one night I had a dream. Two men appeared to me dressed in snow white garments and said: 'Go to the school. There you will be shown the way of life.' So I went to the school and heard you preach. I am now born again. I am a child of God," he smiled.

When the crusade finished Reinhard went back to the school where it had all started to thank the headmaster once again for his kindness and help. As he got out of his car the headmaster came across to greet him warmly: "Pastor Bonnke I'm so glad to see you. I would like to speak to you. Tell me, I am absolutely amazed, how do you manage to do what you do? I have been travelling this area for many years. I know these people. Everything has changed. The whole area is different. My church has had a hospital and mission in the district for 20 years and you have accomplished in seven days what we have been unable to do in all that time. Normally in such mass meetings people make heroes of the evangelists. But the people are not talking about you or Pastor Kolisang. All they talk about is Jesus."

As Reinhard stood opposite the headmaster his eyes glistened because that was one of the finest compliments he had ever received and it so true about his ministry and the work of CFAN. As he and his ministry have grown in stature and as the work has gripped the imagination of tens of thousands of people around the world, he has always maintained that the glory belongs to God and he wants no earthly laurels that fade and decay.

There was a sequel to the huge heap of crutches collected during the Giyani crusade. A picture, showing Reinhard and some of his co-workers holding up some of the sticks and crutches appeared in his missionary newsletter in Germany.

Some German people had been quite critical of the work he was doing in Africa and some even doubted the claims of healings and miracles. The picture should have silenced his critics, but they refused to believe even the evidence of the photograph. In fact, they started the absurd rumour that the leaving behind of walking sticks and crutches was "typical of African people . . . they were absent-minded". When Reinhard first heard this sniping comment he got fairly hot under the collar, but later on he was able to retort: "Blessed is the cripple who forgets his crutches!"

# CHAPTER 13

## Altar call, not protocol!

Undoubtedly the Sibasa Crusade was the high point of 1977 and the huge crowds that came justified Reinhard's decision to get a tent capable of seating many thousands of people. The Sibasa crusade was held in August but at a stage it looked as though it would be cancelled. However, Reinhard was convinced that the Holy Spirit was directing him to have a crusade in that country, which is situated in the far north-eastern corner of the Republic of South Africa, hemmed in by the famous Kruger National Game Park on the east and by a buffer zone which separates them from Zimbabwe in the north.

Application had been made to the authorities for the necessary permits for a four-week crusade in the capital of Sibasa but there was no response and a co-worker ventured the suggestion that if it was God's will to have the campaign then He would open the door. Believing firmly in his heart that it was God's will to go to Sibasa Reinhard's reply showed his keen spiritual perception: "I know God opens doors, but this time the devil is closing it."

The days went by and eventually a reply came: it was a very decisive no, or at least that's what the authorities thought. They did not know that they would have to deal with a very determined and very dogmatic German evangelist, who refuses to see things in the negative. He fumed inside and to make matters worse he came down with a bout of 'flu and forced to rest in bed.

One night he awoke for no apparent reason but when he opened his eyes all he saw in large, beautiful lights was the word SIBASA. "Lord, this is confirmation. Although we have been turned down we will still go," he whispered. As soon as he was well enough he determined to go to Pretoria to see the officials concerned. Arriving in the government building in Pretoria he was delighted to find that the official he was to see was a fellow Christian. Things began to move and permission was granted for the crusade — but for only ten days. But he was rejoicing as he walked along the streets of Pretoria. With him was a newcomer to the CFAN team, Adam Mtsweni, who was in charge of the music ministry and is still with him today. As they walked jauntily through the crowded streets Pastor Mtsweni quipped: "Never mind, God created the world in six days. He can save Vendaland in ten days." A couple of weeks later as Adam led the singing in the Sibasa stadium he could almost believe that his words were coming true.

Being August, dry, cool weather had been anticipated as Vendaland is a summer rain area and Reinhard had hired the Makwarela stadium, in the capital Sibasa, knowing that it might be a bit cool in the evening, but at least it would be clear. They would not have to worry about rain.

But when Reinhard woke up on the first day of the crusade the sky was grey and later on it began to rain — and it didn't stop, but amazingly 200 people braved the wet weather to come out on the opening night.

The main stand had only a small covering over it and an unreliable generator and three floodlights provided the lighting for the meeting. As a precaution Reinhard armed himself with a flashlight to help him read from his Bible. But not only was it wet, but a chilling wind whipped across the vast, open stadium. As he stood in front of his soaked audience he wondered how they could sit so still. His teeth chattered and his limbs shivered in the icy cold conditions.

Worse was to come. The lights blinked on and off and the generator sputtered and died. "It was always a matter of honour with that generator that it failed at least twice during a service," Reinhard laughingly recalls. Realising that his flashlight could be of some assistance to those trying to restart the generator he decided to go down to the bottom of the stands but he missed his footing in the dark and did a gentle cartwheel, landing in a muddy pool of water. Sitting there like a little boy drenched and splattered with mud, he whispered a prayer of thanksgiving for the darkness!

The wet and the cold continued the next day and Reinhard searched the town for hot water bottles for the team but, alas, there weren't any to be found. Not suprising as Sibasa normally enjoyed warm tropical weather all year round. So Reinhard and the team donned extra socks and wore every shirt and jersey they could get over their heads. Amazingly the attendance doubled on the second night to 400. The reason, of course, was that on both nights there were notable healings and the news was spreading. The rain stopped and on the third night the crowd doubled again.

Now the crusade was in full swing and on the seventh night 30 000 people swelled the stadium to capacity. Still there were hitches. The loud speaker system broke down and Reinhard and his interpreter struggled to preach with the aid of loud hailers. Harrassments, yes, but blessings flowed abundantly and large numbers of people came forward each night to make Jesus their Saviour. The stadium erupted with deafening shouts of praise as God's healing power touched people. Co-evangelist, Kolisang was mightily anointed as he prayed for the sick.

One man, on crutches, was prayed for and then threw them away, marvellously healed. He testified that it was his birthday . . . "and what a present the Lord has given me. Now I can walk properly again." The cheering of the crowd made passersby think there was a football match in progress in the stadium! The power of God visited Sibasa mightily and many thrilling miracles and conversions were recorded. Naturally, it was the talk of the town — from the lowliest villager to even the President of Vendaland.

One afternoon while alone praying in his caravan Reinhard received another very clear and precise instruction from the Lord: "Go and buy a beautiful gift for the President of Vendaland." Because there was nothing suitable to buy in Sibasa he drove the 80 kilometres to the town of Louis Trichardt and after hunting through various shops bought an attractive vase. Driving back to Sibasa he mused about how he was going to give the gift to the President as it had never entered into his thinking to visit his offices or to invite him to the crusade. Anyway, the vase, neatly gift-wrapped lay safely on the back seat of his car and he waited to see what would happen next. It came quicker than he ever dreamed.

Hardly had he opened his caravan door when one of the CFAN team came running towards him with an urgent message: the President of Vendaland wanted to see him — that afternoon at 4 o'clock.

"Well, isn't that wonderful. I've got a gift for him. Praise the Lord," he told his colleague. And so everyone hurriedly got into their best suits and, with Bible under one arm, gift under the other, with someone else carrying a piano accordion, Reinhard and some of the CFAN team set off to keep this divinely appointed meeting.

All the members of the cabinet and their wives were at the President's residence when they arrived and the team were ushered into a splendid lounge where about 30 people were seated and waiting. President Mphephu came forward and shook hands and said: "Pastor Bonnke I'm sorry for the problems you have encountered. I have heard that God has blessed my nation through you and your team and I have called you because I also would like to hear what God has to say to us."

Grasping this amazing opening to reach the leaders of the government, Reinhard launched into a typical gospel sermon. He preached as though he had an audience of 500 000 and when he came to the end he knew he couldn't leave the message hanging in mid air. He had to draw in the net, but did protocol permit an old fashion altar call? As these thoughts flashed through his mind the Holy Spirit indicated: "Altar call, no protocol!" So solemnly facing his VIP congregation he said: "Please bow your heads before God and let us pray . . . who wants to give his heart and life to Jesus?" He glanced across at the men and women sitting in the plush lounge and then a hand went up. His heart fluttered — it was that of Chief Mphephu, the president. Then came the Minister of the Interior and the others followed. They probably didn't have any option since the President had given the lead! It was an unusual scene that was played out in the private residence of a head of state as Reinhard and his co-pastors ministered and laid hands on the government leaders. Shouts of "hallelujah" and "praise the Lord" filled the room as salvation came to the leaders of a nation.

The meetings in the stadium reached a tremendous climax and before the close a boyhood vision was recalled. At the closing service Reinhard looked out over the sea of faces — some estimated the crowd at 40 000 — and suddenly he remembered the scene in that home prayer meeting back in Germany when he was 11 years old. The woman had said she saw a little boy breaking bread before a multitude of Black people . . . and here he was, 26 years later breaking the Word of Life to these dear people. The tears welled up in his eyes and he turned aside to weep quietly as he whispered "How great Thou art . . ." Vendaland had been touched mightily by the gospel and a return crusade was planned for early in 1978 — this time with the new tent.

As 1977 closed, the thrilling news for the CFAN team was that the new gospel tent would be ready and in use in 1978.

There was an extra bouyancy in the spirits of the CFAN team as they set off for their first crusade of 1978. The venue was Seshego, Pietersburg, in the Far Northern Transvaal. When the team arrived they caused quite a stir as the fleet of trucks and vehicles, hauling all the equipment and caravans trundled through the town. There was even more excitement as the new tent was raised. It was bigger than any tent anyone had ever seen before, certainly much bigger than a normal circus tent. The seating capacity of the tent was claimed to be 10 000, but this could only be achieved by crushing people onto tiny, narrow benches and this was done on many occasions and even then the crowds overflowed and stood several rows deep around the skirts of the yellow tent.

This yellow tent would, for the next five years, be the "calling card" of CFAN as it criss-crossed southern Africa, going as far north as Zambia. It would become the embodiment of his burning vision to win Africa for Jesus. His course was set and the tent was to be the symbol of this most extraordinary ministry to Africa.

The first crusade in the tent was a wonderful success. It gave a new confidence to everyone not to worry about rain during the services, which often lasted for up to four hours as the people entered wholeheartedly into song and even dancing. For the people of Africa singing and dancing is second nature and the CFAN crusades allow for plenty of that as thousands of voices are raised in praise, worship and adoration.

From Pietersburg the tent trucks rumbled further north for a return crusade in Vendaland — this time in a remote place, called Njelele. Here Reinhard would be severely tested.

# CHAPTER 14

## Demon mountain

When they arrived at Njelele the new yellow tent was pitched and it looked quite regal in its rural setting, but it was also under the shadow of a sinister, brooding mountain. The tent, which had cost R200 000, was the pride and joy of Reinhard and his team. But within a few days the two-month-old tent stood in the middle of a grey, wet and desolate scene. Its sides were mud-splattered and part of the roof was torn and hanging in shreds.

As it rocked and swayed violently in the wind it resembled a battle-scarred ship, listing heavily and about to plunge to a watery grave. Water cascaded down the canvas sides like rampant rapids. Around the skirts of the tent men looked in despair at the cables and pegs that held the tent secure. It was like a swamp and the iron pegs were stirring up giant mud pools. The tent crew, flashlights bobbing in the darkness and driving rain like marker bouys on a stormy sea, looked on helplessly . . . disaster could strike at any moment.

Inside, the glow of the generator-charged light bulbs gave some warmth and comfort to the scene. A hundred faces looked up at Reinhard who was bravely trying to preach a sermon. It was a forlorn scene. These few people had come to hear the gospel, and he refused to disappoint them and carried on, despite the raging storm outside. The audience listened intently, oblivious to noise of the pounding rain and the danger above them.

He had hardly said a final amen after completing his sermon when Eugen Würslin, the then tentmaster, came stamping up the ramp to the platform, leaving a stream of water trickling behind him. Hair plastered on his soaked face he blurted out: "Close the meeting. It's urgent. Please . . . we must evacuate the tent. The pegs cannot hold any longer, and when they go seven tons of steel and cables are going to come crashing down on the audience. It could collapse any moment!"

He looked at Eugen's face. There was fear etched on it. His words dripped with danger. Turning to the audience Reinhard told them simply: "I'm sorry, but we must evacuate the tent. We must close the meeting. We've got to take down the tent."

Even as he spoke the tent crew moved into action. The rain poured down in relentless streams and in between the squalls the wind seemed to breathe horrendous gusts from the direction of the Njelele mountain . . . ancestral home of departed spirits, according to local custom.

When the CFAN team arrived at Njelele they were warned about evil spirits that haunted the mountain which was held to be very sacred by the local inhabitants. A local pastor had told him: "Some time ago a missionary came here and put a tent right where you have put yours. Before he was able to preach one sermon a fearsome wind came down off that mountain and tore his tent to shreds. The missionary packed his bags and left in a big hurry."

Such a threat was, of course, a challenge to Reinhard and he confidently replied: "That will never happen to us."

But now, as he stood in the quivering, battered tent, mud rushing in underfoot, anxious workers barking out orders and the steel masts lurching drunkenly as giant gusts of wind struck the canvas, those bold words of his seemed very empty.

Right from the start the weather had been against them. Tentmaster Eugen had battled day and night to maintain the tent. Sleeping at night was almost impossible as the wind buffeted the caravans. It was like being in a rowing boat on an open sea. Reinhard remembers being woken at 5 o'clock one morning with someone banging on his caravan and as he roused from a fitful sleep he heard words that shocked him awake: "Something terrible has happened. Come and see," said Eugen. Sleepy-eyed he pulled on a raincoat and stepped out of the warmth of the caravan. Immediately his shoes disappeared beneath a muddy morass. Squelching along he followed the tentmaster and as they neared the tent his eyes widened. One of the masts had collapsed and a huge valley had formed in the tent roof. It was filled with 20 tons of water and threatened to bring everything down with it.

As he gazed at the tent, wallowing in a lake of water, it looked like some grotesque monster that had been washed ashore on a lonely beach. He admits that his spirits submerged in despair when he looked around him. All those years of praying and believing God for the tent, all the months of negotiations and work and all that money . . . these were the thoughts that reeled through his mind, but Eugen's urgent voice jolted him back to reality.

"There's only one thing we can do. . ." he was saying . . ."we'll have to slash the canvas and let the water pour through." He looked at the swaying bubble of water and then at Eugen: "Go ahead." It was like passing sentence on an innocent victim.

But the true-grit nature of Reinhárd surfaced — come fire or floods they would go on with the crusade and he made it clear to Eugen:"We are not going to take down the tent. In the Name of Jesus we will continue."

They continued and so did the rain. Roads became impassable, bridges were washed away, but still a few dozen people made it to the tent services.

Up until that moment they had been "limping to victory", but it looked like defeat was now about to overcome them as he watched the tent crew working feverishly to avert a disaster. As he stood watching the scene a man approached him. His face seemed familiar and then he recognized him as Mr Elijah Mulawudzi, who had been saved and healed of a stomach ailment during the Sibasa crusade the previous year. There was a brightness in Mr Mulawudzi's eyes as he looked up at Reinhard and simply said: "Pastor, didn't you preach that all things are possible to them that believe?" The challenge and boldness of the words struck deep inside and they came as a rebuff to his much-vaunted faith. Yes, he had to admit, that was what he preached, and not only that, he also believed it.

"Yes, you are right. I did not only preach it . . . I believe it in my heart," replied Reinhard and as he said the words something began to happen. It was like wakening from a bad dream and realising that all was well. The cobwebs of doubt that had been woven in his heart in the past few days and trapped his faith were blown away as a breath of Holy Spirit power surged into his being. He looked around at the apparently pathetic and helpless situation and then recalled the words of Jesus . . . "All things are possible to them that believe."

The cloud of gloom lifted and like a sergeant major he strode across to the embattled tent crew, who were tugging and straining at ropes and cables. He called them together and told them: "I relieve you of all responsibility if anything goes wrong. In the Name of Jesus I accept full responsibility. This tent is not going to be taken down. We are going to stay here and continue to preach the Gospel."

There was incredulity carved on every face, but the team were touched in their hearts as well. Their faith grew and, inwardly, they knew that it would be all right . . . although their eyes and their minds told them that disaster was less than a raindrop away.

The tent crew carried on with their mammoth task of keeping the tent up . . . or more aptly keeping it afloat! Then, within a short while the miracle happened. The rain stopped and the wind subsided. The hush of silence, after the torrents of rain, brought a quiet peace to the hearts of everyone and a holy awe. "Yes, all things are possible to him that believes," was the thankful prayer of the team as they praised the Lord for intervening when it looked as though a flood would wipe out the crusade.

A resounding victory crusade followed. The sun came out at last from behind an apron of dingy, grey clouds. The muddy ground dried out and then, like an army of ants on the march, the people appeared from over the hills. Down the stony paths and through the open veld they snaked their way to the tent. It was amazing. As the meetings continued there were more people outside the tent than inside it. It was a fantastic triumph for the gospel as the Holy Spirit moved mightily on the people throughout the area.

It was here that Reinhard renewed his acquaintance with the President of Vendaland, Chief Mphephu. This is his traditional residence and he and several other dignitaries came to one of the closing meetings. The President watched in staggering unbelief when 1 500 people were bowled over by the power of the Holy Spirit and began to speak in other tongues. Amazed at what he was witnessing the President had leapt to his feet and exclaimed to Reinhard: "Pastor, what power is this?" Reinhard grinned back: "Your excellency, what you see is the power of the Holy Spirit." Later when the official party of VIPs was leaving, the President called Reinhard aside and earnestly asked him to consider returning for a future crusade.

When it was time to leave and as the trucks creaked and bumped along over the trackless veld, the Njelele mountain was bathed in sunshine. The local people no longer lived in fear. Now they had a new song . . . "Jesus is stronger than the mountain demons . . ." and while he waited in his car Reinhard was confronted with a poignant scene when some village women, suddenly came running out of the bush and knelt in front of his vehicle, begging him not to leave because they had not yet heard the gospel. It touched his heart deeply to realise just how great the responsibility of the commission of Jesus is: "Go ye and preach the gospel to all nations."

Faith won a mighty triumph at Njelele and it was in

this same mood that the next big crusade went on, this time at Mahwelereng, Potgietersrus in April. Night after night up to 5 000 came to the yellow tent and night after night hundreds made decisions to follow Jesus. Like the young man who sauntered down the aisle between the long line of wooden benches inside the tent, paying little attention to the singing and when he saw the White preacher up on the platform hatred and anger welled up inside him.

The man admitted afterwards he had no intention of listening to the sermon, especially when he saw that a White man was the speaker. "Man, when I saw that White skin, all I could think of was murder. I came into the tent to have a look at the girls and to pick out one for myself, but as I looked around a voice suddenly sounded behind me: 'Jesus loves you.' I whirled around, but I couldn't see who had said those words to me. But a sudden change came over me. I suddenly felt as though I was in the presence of God. I thought to myself, 'There is not a single person on this earth who loves me. Who would love me? Jesus?

"I was rooted to the spot. I listened to the White preacher and when he called people forward to give their hearts to Jesus I ran out, tears pouring down my face. Jesus loved me and He died for me."

The young man came forward and when he came onto the platform he threw his arms around Reinhard, hugging him, as hot tears stained his cheeks. It was a wonderful transformation. Just like Paul of old he had been breathing out threats of murder, now he bowed in surrender to the Lord Jesus Christ. The change in his life was instantaneous. He confessed to having seven girl friends and he went to each one and told them his affair with them was over. The last time Reinhard heard from him he was at Bible school, preparing himself to spread the Good News about the love of God. Today he is a minister of the gospel.

Following the Potgietersrus crusade the team headed back to base for a very important date. In between all the campaigning, the purchasing and making of the tent, plans had also gone ahead for the building of an office complex at Witfield. On May 4, 1978 the buildings were officially dedicated. Over 800 supporters and friends of the ministry heard the AFM president, Dr F P Möller, the special speaker, express the opinion that "this evangelistic work would go from strength to strength and would gather momentum." Pastor J W Gillingham, chairman of the CFAN Board, and the committee, all confirmed that they believed that God was preparing them for "one of the mightiest soul-harvests yet." Those views, expressed then, are being dramatically fulfilled today.

Typical of CFAN the festivities didn't last long. Reinhard went on a preaching tour of Germany during May-June and then he was on the crusade trail with a stirring campaign at Namakgale, Phalaborwa, where up to a 1 000 people responded each night to the call of salvation. Then in July he held an evangelistic seminar at Mabopane, Pretoria and, then a very significant crusade at Acornhoek, at a spot called Greenvalley, in the north-eastern Transvaal. It was the arena in which faith and fear would fight out a deadly duel — and there would be only one winner.

# CHAPTER 15

## "Speak to the devil"

The trucks and tent crew went on ahead to set up everything at Greenvalley but while Reinhard was still at the base he received an urgent telephone call from tentmaster Eugen Würslin. He told him that the ground conditions where the tent was being pitched were poor. Everything would be fine — so long as it did not rain. "But if it rains there will be a catastrophe. The whole thing will collapse," warned Eugen, who still remembered the harrowing experiences he had gone through at Njelele. After listening to the tentmaster Reinhard calmly spoke into the mouthpiece of the telephone: "Pitch the tent . . . in the name of Jesus it is not going to rain; it is not going to storm." He didn't realise it at the time but he had thrown the gauntlet down . . . his boldness would not escape a challenge.

When he arrived at Greenvalley he looked around in slight bewilderment at the place where the tent was pitched. He couldn't see anybody except some lean looking goats and sheep. He wondered whether the tentmaster had not made a mistake. But it was no mistake because as the sun dipped behind the moss-green hills the people started streaming down little winding paths, up and down the rolling vales they came, the night air filled with the chatter of thousands of men, women and children making their way to the tent. Attendance was close to 8 000 a night and the response to the gospel was outstanding. By the end of the 17-day crusade over 8 000 people had filled in decision cards. But this great victory was not gained without a struggle, a spiritual struggle that was actually brief in its duration, but stupendous in its outcome, not just for Greenvalley, but probably for Africa.

On the eighth day of the crusade Reinhard was sitting huddled over his Bible in the privacy of his caravan when a blast of wind buffeted the caravan. The sharp sunlight began to get hazy as though a filter were being pulled over the sun and as he stepped out of the van and down onto the grass he looked toward the mountain range in the west. What he saw made him gasp. Black clouds were rolling up over the hills and a fierce wind was pulling the clouds across the sky like huge coils of curly black hair. It looked sinister because the tent stood right in the path of the oncoming storm. There was no doubt that satan had challenged his faith and catastrophe was stampeding towards him in the form of a giant thunderstorm.

As he stood on the grass with the first draughts of the cool, moist wind whipping at his hair, the Holy Spirit spoke to him. This is how Reinhard tells this amazing story.

"The Holy Spirit said: 'Speak to the devil. Rebuke the devil', so I began to stride towards those angry, black clouds. I raised my finger and I shouted: 'Satan, in the Name of Jesus I want to talk to you. Devil, if you destroy this tent of mine I am going to trust God for another one three times the size of this one!'

"My words drifted across the open veld and then something almost unbelievable happened before my

119

very eyes. The wind and the rain parted to the left and to the right, making a wide detour around our tent. The storm never touched us. As I stood there the Holy Spirit whispered to me: 'See, faith frightens satan.'

"I was excited. I had met satan's challenge head-on and he had been defeated by the authority of Jesus. Yes, the devil had been frightened out of his socks! Faith frightens satan. What a wonderful truth. No wonder the Word of God says that our faith is more precious than gold and the shield of faith quenches the fiery darts of the enemy. Yes, faith puts satan and his hellish hordes to flight. Praise God!

"Then as I stood there, a lone spectator of this strange phenomena, which was really a spiritual warfare in heavenly places, a perplexing thought came into my mind. Maybe I had not made myself clear to satan. Maybe there was some misunderstanding. So I raised my voice and boldly said: 'Devil, in the Name of Jesus I want to talk to you once more. Although you withdrew the wind and you withdrew the rain, that doesn't mean that I have made an agreement with you. I WILL STILL BUILD A BIGGER TENT ANYWAY!'

"I needed to make it clear that I did not negotiate any 'deals' with the enemy. For God has told us to cast him out. And that is what I intend to do as long as I live on this earth."

It was an extraordinary incident, something which some people find difficult to understand, how any man could carry on such a conversation with the devil himself. But Reinhard, is not "any man" because that episode displays clearly just how much of a frontline warrior he is in the spiritual battle that wages on this continent and the great trust and confidence he has in his Saviour Jesus and one might humbly add how much the Lord is willing to trust Reinhard.

The challenge also surfaced something that was quietly incubating in his heart — another tent, but no ordinary tent. No, this one would be the biggest tent ever seen on the face of this earth. The seeds of faith for this super gospel tent were sown in the fiery heat of battle at Greenvalley in September 1978. It would take five years before this mighty structure would stand on the soil of Africa, but when it did the rest of Christendom gaped in wonder.

The wind-up crusade of 1978 was to the beautiful mountain country of Qwa-Qwa, which is situated on the northern border of Lesotho. By now CFAN had invested in a 64-seater bus and its main use was to go to schools and bring the children to the tent meetings. During the Qwa-Qwa crusade one particular headmaster refused permission for his pupils to be taken to the meetings because he believed CFAN were some sinister religious sect.

But one young girl sneaked away from the school and went to the tent. She was slightly crippled in one foot and had to wear special shoes. When she reached the tent she slipped quietly on to a vacant spot on one of the wooden benches to hear Pastor Kolisang preach and while she listened a miracle took place — her foot straightened out! She came back the next night and gave her testimony before the 5 000 people in the tent: "God not only gave me a new pair of shoes (she could not wear normal shoes), but He gave me a new heart. I have found Jesus as my own Saviour." She carried that testimony back to her school and shortly afterwards the principal was in contact with CFAN.

"Bring your bus. Please take the children to the meetings," he enthused. It proved to be a breakthrough because during the next few days hundreds of schoolchildren made decisions for the Lord. In fact, whole busloads of children returned to their school hostels saved.

It was during this crusade that Reinhard had a peculiar vision – peculiar in a funny way. God had been manifesting His power mightily in the meetings with multiple healings and thousands responding to the altar calls.

In the vision he saw satan limping around the tent on crutches! and the Holy Spirit said: "See the enemy bears the sign of defeat." For him it was another confirmation for this burgeoning ministry which by now had 32 fulltime members and was expanding all the time. It was a vision he would recall from time to time when it seemed that the enemy was attempting to reverse the roles.

It was toward the end of the year that Reinhard experienced another supernatural vision. In it he saw himself at the helm of a giant battleship. It was a splendid ship. It was heavily armoured and massive guns pointed out over the prow. But as he looked ahead and down to the waterline he noticed that the ship was moving along a tiny river. It was hardly more than a brook and up ahead was a sharp bend. In the vision he turned the wheel madly, but there was not enough water in which to turn and the ship became stuck fast in the mud.

When he awoke from the vision he was puzzled as to the interpretation: "Lord, what does this mean?" In a flash the answer came back: 'That is CFAN.' "I caught my breath and in the stillness of the night I could hear my heart beat a little faster. 'Lord, are we going to get stuck?' Then came the interpretation: 'A ship is carried by water. In the same way Christ For All Nations needs to be carried by holy hands. Your base is too small. You need more holy hands to be lifted up on behalf of this work. Every single prayer partner constitutes one inch of this river. A battleship not only needs firepower, it needs maneuverability if it is to have success in battle,'" he recounts.

It was a timely warning because the next few years would see him and CFAN locked in a deadly spiritual battle as the plan for the giant, new tent began to unfold. Prayer would be the key to the continued success and growth of the ministry. He took immediate steps after this vision to gain more prayer support. A personal letter was sent to his already large number of faithful supporters in which he urged them to "recruit" at least six further prayer-partners for his ministry. Since then he has continually sought more and more people to back him prayerfully and one of the most fruitful ventures in this regard have been mission breakfasts and dinners, which are held in towns and cities throughout the country. By this means he has spread the vision to countless thousands and, as he believes, given Christians the wonderful opportunity to have a real share in CFAN's great mission thrust in Africa.

# CHAPTER 16

## Threatened by satanists

In July-August the crusade venue was a place called Malumelele in Gazankulu. The closest major town to the district is Pietersburg. The trucks rolled in with the equipment and could hardly be seen for the powdery dust that hung in the air. It had not rained in many months but what they found among the people was even worse. It was a spiritual desert, where fear and witchcraft ruled.

Night after night the services were interrupted by people who suddenly let out the most chilling shrieks and even during the day there would be people moaning and screaming as they wandered around the tent. Reinhard and the team got very little sleep because of the sinister mood and the ear-piercing screams that rent the night air. It was like being awake in the middle of a horrendous nightmare. Reinhard recognised that there was a tremendous battle going on in the sphere of the supernatural as the Holy Spirit moved in to set people free. The demonic forces were being provoked and manifested themselves with awful cries.

However, he was still curious to know why so much demon-power was being concentrated around the tent so one day he visited a nearby village. Like most African villages it was a series of lopsided mud huts with grass roofs, but besides the normal dwelling places there were other dwarf-size huts. On examining one of these tiny huts he found it filled with witchcraft fetishes and strange writings. He learned that these huts were in fact shrines, built especially for demon spirits. It seemed to Reinhard that most of the villagers had bound themselves to the demons, but now that they were hearing the gospel they desired to be set free — but the demons were reluctant to leave the victims they tormented and held captive.

The case of one young girl is typical of what happened during this crusade. She eagerly came to the tent to hear the gospel, but as soon as she entered she went into a frenzy. She had appeared quite normal — until she came into the tent. Reinhard and the rest of the team prayed for her, but she could not be released from the evil spiritual powers that possessed her. Pastor Kolisang went home to her hut and, as he suspected, found a large cache of witchcraft fetishes, muti medicines and other sinister looking items. The moment these things were removed and burned the girl became completely free. Before Reinhard left that village he had the thrill of seeing this young girl praising God in a heavenly language when she was baptised into the Holy Spirit.

This experience emphasised something which Reinhard urges all new Christians to do: renounce the past and surrender all the idols and magic potions which may have been a part of their previous life. He has seen over the years that unless the witchcraft fetishes are totally destroyed their owners never seem able to get free of demonic influence.

That is why the platform in the tent is littered with all kinds of objects after an altar call — bits of "holy" ropes, pieces of animal skins, dry bones and many other strange objects are hauled out and turned over.

In his early encounters with demonic forces, Reinhard used to run from one person to the next trying to pray and cast out the demons. "In the crusades I used to be jumping everywhere and I would fall into bed at night, exhausted and I realised that if I continued like that I would not make it to 40. I learnt then to have faith in the Holy Spirit and to let Him move in. The Bible tells us in the book of James that demons believe and tremble and that was clearly shown during the Malamulele crusade."

During the years Reinhard has often been challenged by satanic forces – without even being aware of it. Satanists admit they have deliberately come into the tent meetings with the intention of causing chaos. He was told once that four satanists sat in four different parts of the tent and attempted to call up demons to oppose him while he was preaching, but the demonic powers would not manifest themselves inside the tent. "I was told that the satanist said that the demons raced around the outside of the tent. They could not enter because it was encircled by a wall of fire".

Once, while preaching at the AFM's Maranatha Park, several satanists came into the meeting, again they plotted to oppose Reinhard. The story was told to Reinhard by one of the satanists, who recognised the deception of the devil and surrendered his life to the Lord. With this group of satanists was a witch, highly rated for her ability to cast spells. As she tried to cast a spell she began to shake from head to foot and turning to her companions shouted to them: "Get me out, get me out." One of the satanists, seeing what was happening, reasoned that Jesus is more powerful than Lucifer or any witch, and decided to become a child of God.

Once while preaching in Germany he had a confrontation with a demon-possessed woman. He was midway through his sermon when he distinctly felt a surge of Holy Spirit power in the meeting. A young woman from Switzerland who was sitting near the front suddenly leapt to her feet and screamed. "It sounded as though there were a 1 000 demons in her", recalls Reinhard, and then the woman raced up the aisle and flew through the exit door.

Remembering the incident Reinhard says: "The meeting froze as though somebody had opened a giant fridge and one lady stood up and said: 'Pastor Bonnke, I am dead scared'. Then the Lord spoke to me, 'I have allowed this to happen to demonstrate my power'. I looked at the audience and said: 'How many of you will rise up with me in living faith and command these demons to leave that girl right now? She is outside, but it does not matter because the Holy Spirit is able to minister to her.' The whole congregation rose and in the name of Jesus we rebuked the devil and we took the victory. A few minutes later, the door opened and that young girl came in completely free. That same day she was baptized in the Holy Spirit."

His years of experience in the mission field of Africa have made him fearless when it comes to facing demonic attacks. He's not afraid to mock the devil. Some may see that as bravado, but for him it is a matter of trust and faith in the ability of God. "I'm not afraid of the devil . . . I believe he is afraid of me," he says with a confidence that may take some people aback. One of his oft quoted phrases from the pulpit is: "Faith frightens satan — faith makes us fearless".

He was put to the test in Birmingham, England, in 1981. He received a letter — a very strange letter. It had no name on it and for a signature it had the numbers 666 and some other strange lettering. The letter read: "Bonnke you have invaded our territory. If you don't leave within two days we are going to bring a curse down on your life." Reinhard's reaction was a predictable retort at the devil: "You won't succeed in chasing me. I will chase you out of Birmingham." A few days later he received another letter and when he opened it he saw the 666 sign again. This time he didn't bother to read it, but tore it up and as he tossed the pieces into a bin he remarked: "Devil, I don't read your epistles. I read God's epistles. I am not on the run. The gates of hell are being blasted." He never received any further notes.

# CHAPTER 17

## Healing broken hearts

Following the Malamulele crusade, the team girded themselves up for the next outreach in Mafikeng, which was notable for some outstanding conversions. It also produced this story.

A motorcyclist came speeding down the road, and when he saw the yellow tent and the parked caravans he pulled in and after asking some of the workers, found his way to Reinhard's caravan. The man, in his mid-30s, spoke first: "I was driving along the road on my motorbike when I saw one of your trucks and on the side in big letters was written, 'Jesus heals broken hearts'. Reverend I could not drive on any further. I just had to turn in here to your camp. I didn't want to, but I did. I have a broken heart. Do you think Jesus could heal my broken heart?"

Looking into the man's face Reinhard could see that he had been crying. He asked him in to the caravan and the man poured out his heart.

"Seven years ago I gave my life to God. I found Jesus as my Saviour. I was delivered from all my evil habits and addictions. Then one day my wife went off for a few days to visit her parents.

"I was at a loose end and went for a walk. As I wandered along the street I found myself opposite a place I had visited many times before I met Jesus. I was drawn like a magnet to the place. I couldn't resist it. I stood there wanting to go inside, but I couldn't because I felt the presence of Jesus with me.

"As I stood there I folded my arms and said: 'Dear Lord Jesus, please leave me for just five minutes so I can go in and do what I want to do.' When I came out of that house Jesus was gone and I've been alone with my misery and heartbreak for seven long years.

"Things have gone from bad to worse . . . seven times worse. I am down and out. Crushed. Broken. Do you think Jesus could ever help me again?"

As Reinhard listened and as he looked at the man's pleading eyes his own heart went out to him. He had to help him. He had to do something. Silently he prayed, and then the revelation came. Looking at the man he said: "Listen, I will tell you what to do, and I will help you to do it. I want you to take my hand and walk with me in the spirit back those seven years. Back through the streets of that town and to that place where you prayed that fatal prayer for Jesus to leave you. I want you to kneel down and say: 'Lord Jesus, I revoke that prayer. Forgive me. I revoke that prayer."

Reinhard then knelt down with the man and the man began to shout out his prayer. "Lord Jesus I withdraw, I revoke that prayer, Forgive me!" He wept, but now the tears were not the dregs of bitterness, they were showers of joy. Half an hour later he leapt onto his motorbike, still weeping, but with heaven in his heart. Reinhard returned the wave, then turned to look at the red truck and at the giant white letters: JESUS HEALS BROKEN HEARTS. Yes, it is true.

The closing crusades of 1979 were at Mdantsane, in East London, and at Flagstaff, in Pondoland.

While conducting the East London crusade Reinhard received a nasty shock. He gave an altar call and as the repentant sinners streamed forward he urged them to throw witchcraft objects, liquor and tobacco onto the platform. As he stood there dodging the flying missiles that were hurled up onto the platform he saw something that looked like a thick cable come sailing towards him. The "cables" landed close to his feet and then began to wriggle — they were three poisonous snakes. The danger was quickly averted when song leader Pastor Mtsweni, grabbed the microphone stand , and with the help of some others they clubbed the snakes to death.

Later the man who had thrown the snakes onto the platform gave his testimony. He had inherited the snakes from his parents and he used them for certain witchcraft practices. "But now I want to follow Jesus and have nothing to do with these things anymore." It was another poignant example of the convicting power of the Holy Spirit whenever Reinhard proclaimed the gospel.

Every crusade, of course, has its highlights and everyone of them produces its own characteristics, — for this reason it is difficult to judge which is the most successful, but the November campaign at Flagstaff, must rank as the best of the year.

The crusade lasted 19 days and produced 12 000 decisions for the Lord. The whole area was transformed and, just like in Bloemfontein, the police could vouch for the change in lifestyle. For the whole of the period that the crusade was on there was not a single case of crime reported to the local police station. Thousands made their way to the tent each night, some walking many kilometres, while others came on horseback and cripples were even brought along in wheelbarrows. One of the wheelbarrows produced a remarkable testimony.

One evening, just before the service was to begin, Reinhard noticed a group of people listening intently to one man. The conversation, was of course, in Xhosa, but when the man saw him approach he turned to Reinhard and spoke in English: "I am glad to see you," he said. "Look at this woman here. Every night I have wheeled her to the tent in a wheelbarrow because she was completely paralysed. It was tough work for me because she is so heavy. Now look at her tonight she has walked all the way up that mountain by herself. I never believed there was a God. But now I don't know what to do − I've got to believe that there is a God in heaven and tonight I want to give my heart to Jesus."

Then there was the case of 24-year-old Miss Nokwenzani Mavundla. Four years previously she developed serious headaches. She also suffered swelling in her arms and legs. She was taken to hospital for examinations, but they failed to diagnose the problem and so the parents of the girl decided that the traditional witchdoctor should be consulted. That was the beginning of a nightmare for the young girl. The witchdoctor told the parents that their daughter was changing into a witchdoctor herself and ordered them to slaughter a goat and from part of the skin they were to make a necklace which the girl was to wear.

This was done and then the girl lost her speech. She failed at school and was partly disabled. Friends invited the parents to the tent and they brought their daughter along. She was taken forward for prayer and after Pastor Kolisang had prayed for her he cut off the goatkskin necklace. Immediately a miracle happened and she began to speak and even to sing. She went from one village to another testifying and telling everyone what Jesus had done for her and within nine days she had led 30 people to the Lord. Then she travelled 100 km to the Greenville Mission hospital to tell Dr Kenneth Kaufman, an American missionary and medical doctor, who knew her case history. The staff at the hospital were amazed and were so impressed that they made a special trip to attend one of the meetings.

Another healing that received much publicity in the area was that of Mr John Ncinjane. He had been injured in a mine accident in 1975 and was certified permanently disabled, although he managed to hobble around a bit on a pair of crutches. However, he could not get a job and his wife had gone to work in Durban so as to provide for them and their three young children. When Mr Ncinjane heard about the miracles happening in the tent he came along. On the first night he accepted Jesus as Saviour and joined the healing line, but nothing happened. He came again and again to be prayed for and then one night it happened. He threw down his crutches and walked. It was thrilling for the CFAN team to see this man's bulldog-like tenacity in seeking healing. He was so overjoyed that he walked over three kilometres into the town after the service to telephone his wife in Durban and share with her his miracle.

The healings and miracles drew the crowds, but more important were the thousands who were being born into the kingdom of God. Among the thousands who accepted Jesus Christ were Paramount Chief Justus Sigcau and his sister Stella, both members of the Transkei parliament.

The Paramount chief lived about an hour's drive

away from where the tent was pitched and invited the CFAN team to hold a meeting at his palace. When the altar call was made the Paramount chief and his sister were among the first to respond. He expressed the gratitute of his people for the great tent crusade saying: "The light that CFAN has lit in Pondoland shall spread and glow forever." On the morning of the final Sunday of the crusade the Paramount Chief arrived at the tent service, with a complete entourage, including the Chief of Police, bringing the campaign to a fitting climax.

Besides the crusades of 1979 a new thread was running through the fabric of Reinhard's ministry — a thread that would continue for the next four years and which would dominate his ministry — the Big Tent.

# CHAPTER 18

## The Big Tent

Early in 1979 Reinhard publicly announced through his regular German newsletter and the locally distributed Revival Report his intention to "build a tent three times the size of the present one". The Lord had spoken to him earlier with the words: "This is no longer the day of the sickle, this is the day of the combine harvester." His experience as a crusade evangelist was proof that there was a great harvest of souls to be reaped for the Lord. Besides campaigning in South Africa, he had already made brief visits to Nigeria and Kenya, and seen there the same hunger for the Word of God. These masses of people had to hear the gospel and to reach them would mean using new methods, or adapting old ones to the new situation.

His crusades in the yellow tent drew tens of thousands and he believed that God now wanted him to trust Him for an even bigger one which could seat 30 000 people and, most important, would be a mobile structure.

And so the tent and the vision for Africa unfolded. It began like the gentle murmur of a breeze, until it became a hurricane within Reinhard's heart. He was cautious in the beginning. He knew that the yellow tent had cost R200 000 and now he was considering ordering one that would cost many times that amount. He confesses that as the thought of the size of the project became embedded in his spirit, his mind had to switch off. It was just too much for him to grasp. It was during the crusade at Sebokeng that he was greatly encouraged to go through with the gigantic venture. He was reading in the Book of Romans where it said that Abraham staggered not at the promise God had given him. The thought struck him then: "It's not that we cannot stagger, but that we must not stagger in staggering situations." Enthusiastically he determined then to go ahead with the project. He would not doubt and he would not stagger. He would trust God to provide the money. The incubation period of this divine thought was over. It was time to go to the drawing boards in earnest.

J J Swanepoel, an engineer and dedicated Christian was consulted, and after Reinhard had shared the vision Brother Swanepoel got down to the task of designing the tent. The difficulty, of course, was that there was no existing tent structure on which to model this giant. The size envisaged was far greater than any mobile tent man had ever designed. A huge tent-like structure had been built in the desert of Saudi Arabia, but this was a permanent fixture and in fact, even had air-conditioning in it! From the first drawings a scale model was made. It looked more like a spider's web with cables and ropes suspended from giant poles that encircled the tent. The roof level was low and except for the forest of hanging cables, it looked very much like a conventional tent, and had a huge floor area capable of seating 30 000 people.

Working off this model some financial estimates were made and a figure of R1,5-million was produced. This, according to the estimators, would include transport, electricity and the other ancillaries needed to equip the monster tent. It was also realised that the fabric — at that stage it was believed that normal plastic-type material would suffice — would have to be manufactured overseas. Negotiations began with firms in Hong Kong and in Milan, Italy.

The Italian firm took a keen interest in the project and because of the novelty of it were even prepared to cut their profits, so as to do the job. Bro. Swanepoel made several trips overseas to consult with designers and engineers and in March he was in Milan for talks with the Italians. In the minutes made by Bro. Swanepoel of the meeting it was mentioned by the Italians that they thought it would be possible to erect the proposed suspension tent in six to eight hours, using a work crew of 30. Mention was also made of using up to 1 000 pegs to anchor the tent! As Bro. Swanepoel admitted the following month, after the Italians had suggested some design changes, "It is obvious that we underestimate the size of the engineering feat."

When Reinhard had given the go-ahead for the project he had naively believed that the structure could be designed and delivered within 18 months. In fact, in his Christmas greetings in his magazine at the close of 1979, he wrote: "If God supplies us with the finance for the even bigger tent . . . we will use it in the new year . . ."

# CHAPTER 19

## Across the Limpopo

Reinhard entered 1980 in high spirits. The tent construction was to begin and besides a string of rallies and crusades a special five-month campaign was mapped out for Zimbabwe from mid-June to mid-November.

One of his first major speaking engagements of the new year was at the Johannesburg Renewal Conference, where many churchmen, local and overseas, got an opportunity to hear him and to learn something about his ambitious mission strategy for Africa. From there the first big crusade was at Atteridgeville, Pretoria, followed by one at Tembisa, near Kempton Park. Both these crusades proved tremendously successful with thousands won to Jesus and dozens of outstanding healings reported.

Two noteworthy healings, both involving young girls with back diseases, were recorded in 1980. While ministering at a special AFM meeting at Maranatha Park God performed an outstanding healing before the eyes of the 6 000 people who filled the hall. It involved little six-year-old, Christel Rees, of Benoni, who had been born with a back deformity, which forced her to wear a metal brace.

Her parents had promised to take Christel to the

Maranatha Park meetings so that she could be prayed for. Little Christel told her parents that she believed that Jesus would heal her — if the preacher laid hands on her. So Christel and her parents arrived at Maranatha Park, confident that they would get Reinhard to lay hands on their daughter and pray for her healing. However, when Reinhard finished preaching, instead of calling the sick out he prayed a mass prayer for those who needed healing.

According to Mr Rees his daughter was very distressed and told him straight out: "Jesus and Pastor Bonnke don't love me." Moved by compassion and desperate to see his daughter healed, Mr Rees swept up Christel in his arms and headed for the front of the hall in time to meet Reinhard, who was just coming down the steps. Mr Rees shared his daughter's plight and her desire to be prayed for. So Reinhard prayed and what happened next is best described by Mr Rees: "When Pastor Bonnke started praying there was something like a terrific electric shock-wave going through Christel. It was so severe that it even went through me. A woman, who was sitting nearby, told me that she also felt the shock."

Reinhard then told Mr Rees to take the brace off and so the father went to a nearby room. He immediately saw that a long scar on Christel's back, caused by an operation the previous year in an attempt to straighten her back, had moved to the centre. Grabbing his daughter he ran back into the hall and with tears streaming down his face, walked through the huge crowd triumphantly waving the metal brace high in the air.

Unknown to Reinhard a schoolgirl was also among the congregation at Maranatha Park, who desperately wanted him to pray for her. She was 15-year-old

Esther Langerman, of Germiston, who was also forced to wear a metal brace because of Sherman's disease, which caused her to have a hunch back. Her parents had tried everything that medical science could offer and in a last desperate effort they were saving up enough money to fly their daughter over to America so that a certain evangelist could pray for her. Then they heard about the miracles that the Lord was doing through Reinhard Bonnke and went to the Maranatha meetings, but failed to get him to pray for Esther.

However, they knew he would be speaking the following week at the Johannesburg City Hall and so they made certain that Esther was right in front when the sick were asked to come forward for prayer. The moment Reinhard laid hands on Esther she and her mother both felt "waves of electricity flowing through them". By the time Esther got home and into her bedroom she realised that she was no longer stooping – she was healed. She was taken to the doctor and X-rays were ordered which showed that Esther's back was normal.

The focal point of 1980, however, was Zimbabwe. He had visited there in 1975 at a time when there was still a lot of fighting going on. During that visit he had seen for himself some of the ravages of the war and of the persecution many of the Christians had been forced to endure. Since that time he had been under pressure to hold a crusade there, but had not felt the timing was right yet. Pastors in Harare, hoping to pressure him into conducting a crusade, had even gone so far as to hire a stadium, but Reinhard had still refused to go.

Team members went ahead for the advance planning of meetings in Harare and Bulawayo while campaigns were also organised in various other main centres. Clearance for all the trucks and equipment was arranged at the Beit Bridge border post and the Christ For All Nations convoy for Jesus rolled across the wide Limpopo river.

There was keen excitement among the team as they headed north. Now they were pushing into Africa. Reinhard's vowed intention is to reach Cairo one day with his gospel tent and knowing his determination it would not be surpising to see another kind of "pyramid" nestling in the sands alongside the Nile river before the year 2 000!

In Harare the CFAN team met with local pastors from various denominations who had agreed to join together and support the crusade. These 40 pastors supplied 1 000 workers who assisted with counseling and follow-up work.

After years of armed struggle, there was a real sense of spiritual hunger and Reinhard and his team anticipated great things. They were not disappointed. After only three nights the yellow tent was overflowing. The altar call on the first night had been the biggest he had ever seen, with 3 000 people coming forward to receive Jesus. Reinhard was forced to look for a bigger venue and fortunately the nearby 30 000-seater sports stadium was available. It was mid-winter and the nights were chilly, but this didn't stop the people coming and filling the stadium. The yellow tent was left up so that many people who came from distant areas could use the tent as temporary living quarters. They cooked their meals on small fires outside the tent and turned the bench boards into sleeping platforms at night.

Reinhard's father, lovingly known as "Oupa" to

all the CFAN team, had been staying with his son and was at the crusade in Harare. One night he had a dream and in the morning he couldn't wait to tell Reinhard about it: "Reinhard, I had a dream last night. In it I saw this tent here, but it was empty. There was no one in it. I'm worried that something is going to happen."

Reinhard smiled. He hadn't told his father that they were moving to the stadium! "Don't worry. Your dream is true. There will be nobody in the tent because the meetings are going to be held outdoors."

On the last night of the Harare crusade almost 20 000 attended and Reinhard spoke on the baptism of the Holy Spirit. Some 5 000 people came forward to receive Him and what a night it turned into as waves of Holy Ghost power swept through the crowd. The night sky was filled with the voices of thousands praising in a heavenly tongue. Many lay on the ground oblivious to anything that went on around them. It was a day of Pentecost for Harare.

The crusade received prominent coverage on the radio and television and Reinhard was able to appear several times on TV as the media got excited about the huge crowds which flocked to the gospel meetings. While in Harare he had the opportunity of speaking at the University of Zimbabwe, where 500 students turned out to hear him.

From Harare the crusade moved to Bulawayo and again there were great crowds and great triumphs for the Lord.

Reinhard recalls fondly the story of a young man who was found weeping bitterly outside the tent. "He approached one of the counsellors and asked: 'Why am I not accepted in there?' he asked pointing toward the tent. 'Those people inside there hate me.' Sitting down with the man, the counsellor soon got to the bottom of the problem.

"The man was being heavily convicted of sin and felt that God would not accept him. The love and the way of salvation were explained to him. Within minutes he was inside the tent rejoicing and praising God. He had experienced the forgiveness of God."

Then there was Mrs Ethne Pettifor who was brought to the tent by her husband and two teenage daughters. She was in desperate need. For 18 years she had been tormented with a seizure that caused her to grind her teeth, lose her speech and jerk her arms grotesquely. She was prayed for and then came back again the next night. Then a team member visited her home and spent several hours in prayer and counseling until total victory was brought to Mrs Pettifor and she was completely cured.

A school headmaster, Mr C P Ngwenya, gave this eye-witness account of the crusade in Bulawayo: "When advertisements went out about the crusade, people were not over impressed. We had heard before about so-called miracle workers, but nothing happened.

"But after Pastor Bonnke preached the Word it was clear that he was endued with power. The demonstration of the power of God through healings and salvation stunned the multitudes.

"I saw drunks giving their lives to God. Drug addicts throwing away their drugs and cigarettes. Witchdoctors denouncing the profession and throwing their 'magic medicines' onto the platform . . . an experience never seen here before."

From Bulawayo the crusade moved on to Mutare

(formerly Umtali), a pretty little town nestling in the greenery of the Eastern Highlands.

While in Mutare, Reinhard and the team held prayer meetings in a house in the town. When they gathered together for a prayer meeting it sometimes became a bit noisy — they certainly never whispered their joy and praise! One day, while they were praying someone came to the door with a note from the house across the road. Reinhard thought they were in for a rebuke because of the noise. When he opened the note he read: "I am a Christian and I was sick in bed the other day when I heard your prayers and praises, and while I listened God touched my body and I was healed." Needless to say the team raised their voices to an even higher pitch of praise!

Of course, behind the scenes all through the year the new Big Tent was making progress — slowly. Tests were carried out on the circular model and it proved unsatisfactory in high wind. So it was back to the drawing boards. The round tent now became an oblong tent and an extra 13th mast was included. This mast later caused problems and was ditched. A leading engineering firm in America, Messrs Geiger & Burger Associates, were now working in close co-operation with Bro. Swanepoel, who flew to America several times during the year. The re-designing held up construction, but Reinhard, ever the optimist, was still hoping to have the tent up the following year.

Costs, in the meantime, had started to climb, mainly due to inflation, but also because of the high cost of the new membrane. In 1980 it was estimated that the material would cost R150 000. However, although the membrane was going to cost more the engineers felt very much happier using this new glassfibre cloth, covered with silicone rubber. It does not stretch and is admirably suited to the tension structure design of the tent. Financially, prayer partners in Germany and South Africa had faithfully supported the Big Tent project and Reinhard reported in his magazine that half of the R1,5-million needed had already been given.

It was also becoming clearer just how much ancillary equipment was going to be needed to make the Big Tent fully functional for crusades. Most prominent among these was transport. Back in 1980 engineers estimated that 10 or 12 trucks, would be needed to transport the structure from site to site. The final count on trucks today is 19, and they alone, cost R1,5-million.

But for the time Reinhard was not concerned with the accessories, all he wanted was to see the tent standing. Fortunately, the veil is drawn on the future because it was not until December 1982 that the tent stood for the first time. Although the tent design had been finalised the enormity of the structure and the time scale needed to finish it had never really been calculated by anyone. The task was one that would tax the best engineers in the world. There was no exisiting structure which could be copied. This was a pioneer project. It was like trying to design a cavernous sports stadium and then folding it up all neatly, putting it carefully into cargo containers, unpacking it at another venue and putting it all together again. Some of the engineers had to admit later that there were times when they doubted that it could ever be achieved because of the immense size involved.

But as the year closed Reinhard was confident that mid-1981 would be the Year of the Tent . . .

# CHAPTER 20

## The Soweto witchdoctor

Reinhard does not believe in resting on past victories. Like a general commanding an army he savours the triumphs for the moment, but doesn't get sedated by the heady aroma of success. He's always planning ahead for the next skirmish, plotting to plunder hell further and never allowing himself to be ambushed by doubts or walking into a minefield of pride. He looked back on 1980 with a thankful heart, for during the year's many crusades, rallies and other meetings at least 100 000 people came to know Jesus as Saviour. For 1981 he had a campaign mapped out that would see even greater conquests gained for the kingdom of God.

Following up on the great success of the extended crusade in Zimbabwe, a five-month campaign to Zambia was scheduled for the latter part of 1981. Before that, though, there was to be a stupendous return to Soweto.

But the first major crusade of the year was in the mining town of Welkom in the Free State and it was a 24-carat gold event. Thousands of miners, who spent most of their working days buried deep in the bowels of the earth, experienced something of heaven as a powerful Holy Spirit anointing swept through the meetings night after night. The climax of the crusade was a meeting in the Welkom Ice Rink when a multiracial crowd of 5 000 joined together to praise God.

One beautiful testimony that came out of Welkom was that given by a 13-year-old boy, Daniel Motaung. From birth his eyesight was poor and as he grew older so his sight deteriorated. He wore glasses, but they didn't help very much and after a medical examination he was told that the nerves in his eyes were damaged and that he would eventually lose his sight completely. While shopping with his mother in a Welkom supermarket one morning an unknown White man came up to young Daniel and told him about the crusade in the yellow tent and about the miracles that were happening each night. He urged Daniel and his mother to go to the meeting.

His mother, Mrs Miriam Motaung, was not keen on the idea, but young Daniel begged her to take him to the meeting. They went and when Pastor Kolisang laid hands on Daniel he suddenly received his vision. Daniel's first comment after this wonderful healing was: "Now I can study without any problem." Naturally, news of the supernatural healings spread quickly among the tightly-knit mining community and the crowds multiplied.

It also spread to the White community and one day Reinhard was asked to visit a very sick woman in the suburb of Riebeeckstad. The woman, who belonged to the Dutch Reformed Church, had been ill for the past ten years and when Reinhard met her she weighed 27 kg. She was so frail that her 12-year-old daughter carried her around the house because for the past two years she had been unable to help herself.

When Reinhard saw the pathetic bony frame,

covered with a papery covering of skin he realised that she was on the point of death. Yet, when he asked her if she was a child of God she beamed broadly and when he asked her if she believed that Jesus could heal she nodded as firmly as she could and said: "Yes, I believe with all my heart." Reinhard sensed a high level of faith in the woman and there was a spirit of joyful anticipation in the room. "I started to pray for her," recalls Reinhard, "and as I did I felt the hands of that Great King come down upon me." A couple of weeks later he received a telephone call in his office at Witfield. It was the woman's pastor: "Do you remember that lady at Riebeeckstad? I rejoice to tell you she is around and about and she even does her own shopping." It was another bouquet for the Lord.

From Welkom the main focus fell on Soweto. He had received many calls in the past urging him to hold a campaign in this "city" within the city of Johannesburg. But each time he had gone to the Lord in prayer he had received a negative answer. He waited patiently for the right time. That time was March and there was no doubt that it was right on schedule because the welcome and the response from the people of Soweto was overwhelming and after a three-week break the crusade continued for another two weeks in April/May. God's hand was placed firmly on Soweto.

Ever since the pioneering bicycle campaign in Soweto in 1975 Reinhard had believed that one day he would return to hold a full-blooded crusade. The yellow tent was pitched next to the Jabulani stadium. Around them were a myriad of small houses and each evening and morning the air was shrouded in dense smog from a 100 000 chimneys. In 1981 electric street lighting was not yet installed and local pastors had warned Reinhard not to expect very big crowds.

The opening nights were quiet. The crowds were small, and Reinhard admits that he was a bit disappointed at the time. Then the breakthrough came and when it did it was spectacular. This time it was not a physical healing.

A sangoma, 66-year-old Pauline Mbatha, who had ruled as the chief witchdoctor in Soweto for ten years, and whose influence had spread beyond the borders of South Africa came to the tent one night.

When Reinhard gave his altar call Mrs Mbatha shuffled down the aisle and stood directly in front of Reinhard. Strings of beads, all significant to her art of witchcraft were entwined around her colourful dress. As she looked up into Reinhard's eyes she called out for a knife. "Give me a knife. I want to cut this all off," she pleaded as she tugged at her many witchcraft fetishes. A knife was produced and some of the pastors helped to cut off the beads and goatskin bracelets she wore.

The congregation, meanwhile, stared in unbelief — here was a servant of satan surrendering to Jesus. It was a signal to the people of Soweto, and her conversion to the Lord spread like wildfire among the thousands of workers who travel in by train to Johannesburg each morning. Although the population of Soweto is highly sophisticated when compared with the rural districts, the sangoma, or witchdoctor wields just as much power and influence as those in the remote village kraals. So with such a prominent sangoma accepting Jesus Christ, the curiosity of Soweto was acutely aroused. The night following Mrs Mbatha's conversion the tent was almost filled to capacity. People were getting saved by the hundred and physical healings were taking place nightly. The next night it was jammed full and the crowd overflowed and, just like it had happened in Harare, Reinhard moved next door into the football stadium.

The dark, unlit streets of Soweto, were alive with people praising the Lord and the muggers and thieves seemed to melt away. Whites, who were normally too afraid to venture into Soweto after dark, also turned up. Local church leaders were astonished and thrilled as thousands were swept into the Kingdom of God. Miracles and healings abounded. Deliverance from demonic forces occurred at every service and victory was the keynote as the wind of the Spirit refreshed and revived Soweto.

The saving of the witchdoctor, Mrs Mbatha, was indeed the key that opened Soweto to the gospel. And the story behind her coming to Christ is a glorious one.

Mrs Mbatha had not been a witchdoctor all her life. However, she explained that shortly after her husband died she had experienced a strange, supernatural phenomena. He had "appeared" to her in visions and instructed her to become a witchdoctor. For a while Mrs Mbatha had tried to resist these evil spirits, but she had become dangerously ill. Visits to doctors and to hospital were in vain. Because of her bad health Mrs Mbatha did the only thing she thought she could — she submitted to the evil spirits. The very next day, after making this decision she was visited by a witchdoctor from Durban, 600 km away, who claimed he had been sent by the ancestral spirits to help prepare and train her.

Mrs Mbatha became an extremely good pupil and

very "gifted". Her "powers" were quite astonishing and people came from all parts of the country to visit her to receive cures.

Unknown to Mrs Mbatha one of her daughters, Mrs Ruth Pefile, had come under the sound of the gospel and gave her heart to the Lord in 1977. "From the time my mother became a witchdoctor I was uneasy. I knew it was not right. Then I got saved and began to pray and fast for my mother's salvation."

When the tent had been pitched next to Jabulani stadium Ruth and her husband attended one of the first meetings. Ruth decided to invite her mother. "I didn't want to come to the meeting," Mrs Mbatha told Christian workers afterwards, "I did not believe in the things my daughter did." However, Ruth was a persistent daughter. "I begged her. 'Just one meeting. That's all,' I pleaded."

Heeding her daughter's pleas she went to the tent. "When I saw my mother go forward when the altar call was given I cried for joy and thanked God. I had wept many tears before the Lord for my mother. God was faithful. Now I have a new mother," said Ruth at the time.

To prove to the world that her past was wiped out and her sins forgiven Mrs Mbatha voluntarily threw away and burned all her dry bones, medicines, herbs and other black magic charms. It made a huge bonfire and was gloriously publicised by a local Sunday newspaper with a front page picture of the fetishes going up in flames.

It was a remarkable testimony of God's grace and of the power of God to not only challenge the forces of darkness, but to bring light and life into a life that was ruled by fear and evil spirits. Mrs Mbatha, later visited the CFAN headquarters, and she and her daughter had joyfully joined together in fasting and praying for the salvation of their family, many of whom were bound by the curse of ancestral spirits.

Reports of healings and of conversion were many, but one of the most poignant scenes amidst all the shouting and praising involved a mother, whose name is now forgotten, and her daughter. The woman had gone blind at the birth of her daughter. She was led to the front of the tent by her daughter, who was now 11 years old. Pastor Kolisang prayed for her and she regained her eyesight while she stood there. In a touching, reverent scene she turned to look at her daughter — for the first time. Tears stained the cheeks of mother and daughter as they went home that night.

The esteemed Pastor Sipho Bhengu, said of the crusade that in his 23 years of evangelising, he had never seen anything quite like what was happening in Soweto. One Saturday night over 3 000 people came forward to receive the baptism in the Holy Spirit and it looked as though a giant wave had swept through the stadium as people were knocked off their feet. Miracles, physical and spiritual, were the only topic of discussion and once and for all Soweto knew that Jesus is alive.

It seemed a pity to have to end such a tremendous campaign, but the team was scheduled to move on to Malawi, however this crusade fell through and so after a brief rest Soweto II was launched. The second phase of the crusade was held in the tent because of the colder weather and still the crowds came along. Indeed, the 1981 Soweto crusade brought amazing transformations to thousands of lives, like the simple story of Simon Kluswayo, who at 48 years of age, had never been inside a church. He gave his life to the Lord one night and was able to give this decisive testimony later on: "When I accepted Jesus I felt a heavy burden rolling off my chest. Now I love the Lord and I want to know more about Jesus."

Then there was the startling confession of a minister, Rev Maurice Makape — he wasn't born again! He discovered that after he visited the tent. "I was on my way home when I saw the tent so went inside to see what was happening. The Word of God pierced my heart. It was as though I was looking into a mirror and that mirror reflected all my sins." He accepted Jesus as his personal Saviour and then kept coming to the meetings to learn more about the way of salvation. "I am determined to preach a new message to my church. Now I will preach the truth," he said.

On May 10, 1981 the final service of a truly sensational crusade ended. The tent came down, the masts were loaded up and the trucks rumbled along the streets and back to the Witfield headquarters — but Reinhard would be returning for a third time and then he would bring with him the world's largest tent.

# CHAPTER 21

## Preachers' graveyard

For four weeks in May and June Reinhard was in Germany, preaching to his own people and inspiring them with his vision for Africa and, of course, the Big Tent. Construction of the tent was continuing and things were beginning to take shape, but the end was still far away.

The site where the factory had been constructed was proving too small and a neighbouring plot of ground, costing R83 000, had been bought. In a newsletter to prayer-partners on the eve of his departure to Germany he wrote: "The construction of the new tent is well under way. Until today the Lord has graciously supplied our needs so that we are able to weld and work as fast as we can. My policy is, and remains, that we are not taking loans from banks or private individuals, but trust God, to whom silver and gold belongs . . . our target date for the opening of the new tent is March 1982, or earlier. I believe God for a further million miracles to make this possible."

During the first quarter of the year the first shipment of the new membrane arrived at the Springs factory and the steel work was going ahead on schedule, but unknown to Reinhard there was no way the 1982 deadline was going to be met either.

The financing of the Big Tent has been a miracle

right from its earliest beginning and while in Germany in 1981 Reinhard was speaking at a place called Karlsruhe. He had taken with him a brochure and there was also a model of the Big Tent in the foyer of the auditorium. He shared his vision with the people for the tent and for Africa and made it very clear that he was not there to beg for money. "I don't ask for money. I pray for it," he told them. Throughout his ministry he has always emphasised that if people did give money to the project they were not giving it to him – but to God.

During the meeting there was a message in tongues and in the interpretation the Lord said: "I will give a sign today." Sitting in a chair on the platform Reinhard knew that the message was mainly to do with signs of healing and deliverance and was directed at the congregation, but he whispered a hurried prayer: "Lord you know I need a sign as well." There were financial pressures back home because the tent project had an insatiable appetite for money.

After the service Reinhard was standing in the foyer when a woman approached him. This is what she told him: "Last year when you ministered here I found Jesus as my Saviour. Now God has told me to give you some money for your new tent. I was sick at home and I could not get to this conference. Last night I had a dream. I saw you stand and wave. I jumped out of bed, got into my car and here I am, and here is a cheque for R50 000."

With that she disappeared while Reinhard stood open-mouthed, gaping at the cheque in his hand – it was the biggest single donation, till then, that he had ever received. Truly, it was a sign for the tent!

At a meeting in Hamburg, during the same year,

Reinhard used some strongarm tactics to help a woman gain an amazing physical healing. A young Dutch woman, Miss Edith van der Werff, came forward on crutches. She told him she had been involved in a car accident and that a nerve in her left leg had been severed. Doctors said she would never walk again without the aid of crutches. Looking in her eyes Reinhard asked a simple question: "Do you believe all things are possible to them who believe in Jesus?" She said she did and then he prayed for her.

"The moment I laid my hands on her I felt a mighty flow of the power of God surge through my hands. I said to her: 'Sister you are being healed". She said: 'Pastor didn't you understand, the nerve is cut.'

"But didn't you believe that Jesus is able to do miracles?" She agreed, but then added: "But I can't walk without the crutches."

Then Reinhard did something that he'd never done before — he took her crutches away. "I have the witness in my heart that you are healed right now. Walk in the name of Jesus!" The woman took a few tottering steps and began to walk. The next morning she telephoned Reinhard to tell him she was running up the stairs. Later, when he got back to South Africa, he received a letter from her in which she wrote: "Dear Pastor Bonnke, I thank God that you took my crutches away." Looking back Reinhard says: "God forgive me for pulling her crutches away, but it was the right thing to do."

During 1981 Reinhard made three other overseas visits — to England, where he and Pastor Kolisang held some stirring meetings in the City Hall in Birmingham, and then he went alone to Toronto, Canada, and also to Calcutta, India.

His visit to Toronto caused an unusual stir among Canadian Christians. He was invited to be a guest on the famous "100 Huntley Street" Christian television show which is beamed daily from their Toronto studios. He and David Mainse, head of the TV station, immediately struck a friendship and for four days Reinhard was on screen while extracts of the newly-released CFAN film "Africa shall be Saved" were shown.

The cuts from the film created great interest and on the day that an extract was shown of a multitude of people receiving the baptism in the Holy Spirit, Reinhard felt moved to pray for viewers to receive the baptism as well. Within minutes the 25 telephones, manned by trained counsellors were jammed as hundreds of Christians called in to joyfully tell of not only receiving the gift of the Holy Spirit while watching the programme, but of also being "slain" in the Spirit.

The presenter of the German programme was so impressed with the work that Reinhard was doing in Africa that he gave him an unprecedented opportunity to make an appeal to the Christians of Canada. For some preachers that opportunity may have set the cash register bells ringing in their minds, but not Reinhard. His appeal, as usual, was firstly spiritual: "Pray for me. Pray for our ministry and pray for the lost souls of Africa." When Reinhard stepped out of the glare of the lights and was back in the control room he remembers this thought flashing into his mind: "You fool, why didn't you ask them to PAY not pray." But Reinhard felt that his decision had been the wiser one and that his integrity before man and his trust in God, were worth more than a sugary commercial for money. Nevertheless, David Mainse raised $30 000 by an appeal and presented it to Reinhard.

His basic reason for going to Calcutta was to briefly visit his sister Felicia, who after qualifying as a nurse, had met and married an Indian doctor, Ronald Shaw. The couple now work at Mark Buntain's famous mission in Calcutta.

Before he arrived in Calcutta he had been warned that this city of starving and dying millions, was also the graveyard of great evangelists. Reinhard's reaction was typical of the unruffled confidence which he always portrays: "Well, I don't have to worry . . . I'm not a great evangelist."

When he was fetched at the airport his hosts asked him whether he could "feel the oppression and the evil in the air."

"No," he replied. "I don't because I come in the name of Jesus." As always he only sensed victory.

He was invited to preach in one of the city's biggest Pentecostal churches, which seated about a thousand people. Again his hosts warned him: "Don't expect anything great. We don't see miracles. We don't know why, it must be this oppression which hangs over the city."

Not being a man to rub shoulders with Doubting Thomas' Reinhard went to his room to be alone with God and to pray: "Lord, they say they don't see miracles here, that's why I want to see miracles here in the name of Jesus."

When Reinhard strode into the church he sensed no evil, except the scent of battle. It was something like a duel and Reinhard knew the role he had to play. He didn't waste any time parrying with his opponent, but went straight on to the offensive — he preached on faith. Within a short while there were triumphant "hallelujahs" ringing through the church. Like a fighter with his opponent on the ropes Reinhard knew he had hell's forces in a knot. As he came to a victorious close he called for the sick to come forward, and then asked specifically for the blind to come out first. The stage was being set again for a Mount Carmel duel.

An elderly woman was ushered forward. In Reinhard's own words she was "as blind as a stone". He learned later that she was a "regular customer" for all visiting preachers. As the woman was led forward Reinhard whispered to himself: "O, God, this is the moment . . ." With every eye in the church focussed on the little huddle of people at the front Reinhard laid his hands on those dead eyes and prayed: "In the name of Jesus Christ, the Son of God, blind eyes open."

He stepped back and then the woman started to scream: "I see, I see . . ." The pastors of the church began to rejoice and there was a move of the Holy Spirit in that building which reminded him of the waves of power he had become used to in the tent back in southern Africa.

When he boarded his flight home Reinhard had proved once again: God can do miracles anywhere and He's never stopped performing them.

On the plane the man who was now so accustomed to preaching to massive crowds got the opportunity for some old fashioned one-to-one witnessing. He found himself sandwiched between a South African, who had an unquenchable thirst for Cape wines, and a stoic-faced Chinese. He spoke to the South African about Jesus, but he was not receptive and the Chinese man was silent. So Reinhard decided not to press on any further and dozed off.

When he awoke the silent Chinese man was gone and in his place was a young businessman from Taiwan and Reinhard was soon engaged in conversation and they spent several hours talking about Jesus. By the time they parted company at Jan Smuts airport the businessman was asking how to receive Jesus and Reinhard invited him to come to his house for dinner. After dinner the two knelt down and the man, brought up as a Buddhist, accepted Jesus Christ as his personal Saviour.

# CHAPTER 22

## Shaking a nation

The motto of Zambia, the copper-rich country that shares the famous Victoria Falls with Zimbabwe, is One Zambia, One Nation.

After the Christ For All Nations five-month campaign in 1981, the authorities could well have changed the slogan to One Zambia, One Saviour — Jesus!

Reinhard and his team campaigned in the major towns of Livingstone, Kabwe, Ndola, Kitwe and, of course, the capital, Lusaka. There were dramatic results from this marathon campaign. Results which have stood the test of time because 18 months after those giant crusades CFAN team members went back to Zambia on holiday and met scores of people who were still talking about those astonishing meetings.

Reinhard decided to go to Zambia because it was another link or extension of his vision for Africa and it gave the team practical experience in conducting campaigns of such length and at such long range from home base. Something which will become common once the Big Tent begins its gospel safari across Africa.

The convoy of vehicles was most impressive when it rolled out of Witfield. It was a long haul to Zambia as the fleet of caravans and red and white trucks headed out on the Great North road, across the Limpopo, through Zimbabwe and then across the Zambezi river and into Zambia. The distance was over 1 800 km. But every kilometre travelled was worth a precious soul.

During the arduous drive, Pastor Kolisang experienced some trouble with his vehicle and had to make an emergency stop at a garage on the Harare-Sinoia road in Zimbabwe.

Kolisang was driving the Bible shop van, which was loaded almost down to its axles with Bibles and other Christian literature. The van limped into a roadside garage and Kolisang asked a mechanic to examine the vehicle to see how serious the damage was.

He was worried about the cost of the repairs, so before the work was started he asked for a quote. The garage owner looked at Kolisang and told him: "There's no charge for you. The repairs are free." Kolisang was amazed. That was not the way garages usually operated! The garage owner then explained: "I have a brother and he went to hear Pastor Bonnke preach when CFAN held crusades in Harare. My brother was a hopeless drunkard. But he gave his heart to the Lord and now he is well and serving Jesus. Now God has given me this opportunity to return thanks for saving my brother. That's why there's no charge."

That set the tone for the campaign as door after door swung open and the impact pulsated into every segment of the society, until the meetings became national news.

The newspapers and television service gave wide coverage to the crusades, despite a slightly cynical approach at first. One reporter admitted while interviewing Reinhard that he believed in neither the devil nor God, but he had been forced to re-think the matter after seeing a woman, whom he personally knew was blind, walking unaided through the streets of Lusaka completely healed.

A television crew pitched up at the Lusaka crusade to film the service and to catch the drama of the sick being healed. They were not disappointed because they were able to film for all to see how God healed a blind woman and how hundreds responded to the altar call. The cameras vividly caught the tear-stained sinners making peace with God.

During one moving service Reinhard turned to one of the television crew and said to him: "My friend have you given your heart to the Lord?" With tears in his eyes the cameraman looked up at Reinhard and said: "I've done it already, pastor. Two nights ago I was born again."

During the Ndola crusade a young woman came forward and gave her heart to Jesus. She was just one of many thousands whom Reinhard never met. But he heard later a tragic, yet warming story, of what that decision had meant for that young Zambian woman.

Rosemary Mtemwa, 23, was the daughter of a local magistrate in Ndola. She was studying psychology at the University of Zambia, in Lusaka, and while visiting her parents in Ndola she and her parents and her three brothers, came to the CFAN tent.

Rosemary opened her heart to the Lord and she and her family experienced the baptism in the Holy Spirit. Young Rosemary was overflowing with happiness and everywhere she went she told people about her Saviour and how much she wanted to follow Him all the way.

Rosemary bought a CFAN T-shirt from the book

shop with the inscription, "I belong to Jesus" written on the back of it. She wore it every day to prove to all that she was Jesus' property. But when Rosemary confronted her boyfriend with her Saviour there was a violent reaction. Rosemary told him that the Lord had forgiven her sins. She now had a new life and no longer appreciated his sexual advances. The boyfriend flew into a rage, picked up a broken bottle and attacked her. A main artery was severed as he lunged at her and Rosemary died in a pool of blood, wearing the T-sheet which confirmed her testimony: "I belong to Jesus".

God did a wonderful work of grace in the hearts of Rosemary's bereaved parents. Her mother said: "Rosemary no longer belongs to me, but to Christ and He has the right to take her away. I was comforted by God's Word, and instead of crying I have a deep, heavenly joy in my heart because of Him."

Going through Rosemary's private papers, her parents found a notebook in which was penned the scripture: "Rejoicing in hope; patient in tribulation; continuing instant in prayer." Romans 12:12. She had written it down only a few days before she met her sudden and tragic death.

Her life on this planet for Jesus was indeed very brief. But her testimony lives on.

A dramatic moment occurred at the Lusaka crusade when a 13-year-old boy, Judson Banda, deaf and dumb from birth, was miraculously healed. The boy's parents had sought medical aid for many years. When the father Mr Hudson Banda, a building contractor in the city, heard about the miracles in the tent he went along. He surrended his life to Jesus and was born again and the following night he brought his deaf and dumb son to the tent and God did the miracle.

Testimonies similar to this were heard each night and while in Lusaka Reinhard was invited to preach on Zambia Television. He was able to announce an address for people to write into and within days they were flooded with letters from all parts of the nation. A teacher, who had watched the TV transmission of his message, told the following story:

"I was sitting in my lounge at the college watching your programme when suddenly there was a banging on the door and a group of our matric pupils burst in pleading to be allowed to watch on my TV because their's had just broken down. They came in and before the programme was finished they were on their faces crying to God for forgiveness and mercy."

The television studio had also been inundated with telephone calls, and so he was invited to return for a further interview and another preaching session. It was because of this outstanding response to his preaching over the television that an entire outside broadcast unit was sent to the tent site to film the crusade live.

The Lusaka newspaper, **The National Mirror**, carried a prominent report and interview on the crusade and even wrote an editorial, which was proudly brought back to Witfield when the team returned. It read:

"CFAN is fulfilling the message of nearly 2 000 years ago when Jesus said: 'Go ye into all the world and preach the gospel to every creature . . . and these signs shall follow them that believe. In my Name they shall cast out devils . . . they shall lay hands on the sick and they shall recover.'"

"Indeed miracle healing is being witnessed. On the second day of the two-week crusade four blind people received their sight. The following day two people left their crutches behind . . . and scores of others had demons cast out of them. The power of God was certainly at work."

"It is for this reason that we take this opportunity to thank all those who made it possible for evangelist Bonnke and his colleagues to come to Zambia. To them and to CFAN, we say God bless you all!"

- EDITOR, National Mirror, Zambia, July 17, 1981.

That editorial proved that some newspapermen do have a heart of flesh under the usual breastplate of chilling cynicism that is so characteristic of journalists.

All this glaring publicity on televison, radio and in the newspapers couldn't help but penetrate into the highest office of the land. In State House, President Kenneth Kaunda, had also been aroused by this fiery German speaker, who was turning his capital city upside down. A local preacher and friend of Reinhard, Pastor Traugott Hartman, who was one of the main organisers for the Zambia campaign, twisted some arms in the corridors of power and got the CFAN team an audience with President Kaunda. The invitation to come to State House arrived while the CFAN team were in Livingstone on the last leg of the country-wide campaign.

It was an exciting moment as Reinhard, Bible under arm and accompanied by co-evangelist Kenneth Meshoe, CFAN's latest recruit David Beard, a photographer from America, and Pastor Hartmann drove up to State House. Reinhard also carried a gift-wrapped silver candlestick, which he presented to President Kaunda.

When they arrived they were escorted into a beautiful private study-sitting room, surrounded with bookcases and furnished in Louis XIV period chairs.

When President Kaunda entered Reinhard told him what God was doing in Zambia and also in South Africa and he told him about the recent crusades in Soweto and in Bloemfontein. According to Reinhard, the President was fascinated, as he expounded to him the things of the Lord. They never got on to politics, "we just talked about Jesus", recalls Reinhard and then he shared a Bible reading from the book of Proverbs, chapter 21, verse one: "The king's heart is a stream of water (or irrigation canal) in the hand of the Lord; He turns it wherever He will." When they were through President Kaunda turned to Reinhard and asked: "Will you pray for me?" and as they bowed their heads in the plush surroundings of the study a "mighty anointing came down," to use Reinhard's recollection of the prayer. Reinhard left State House deeply impressed by President Kaunda.

"He is open to the things of God. We spoke briefly about the miracles that God performed and the attitude of people to them. He commented: "If you don't believe it (miracles) then you won't see them." His parting remark to Reinhard after their 45-minute interview had been: "Please come back to Zambia.".

The final act of the Zambia campaign was played out at Livingstone, within sound of the magnificent Victoria Falls. It was a fitting place to end this triumphant tour because the blessings flowed in a torrent and for several nights there were more people outside the tent than inside it. The two weeks at Livingstone resulted in over 11 000 decisions for Jesus.

It was a weary team that returned to Witfield in December for a well earned rest. All the while they had been away the tent project had been making progress. Maybe not as fast as Reinhard would have wished, but he was still predicting that it would be ready for use in 1982. A morale-booster was the raising of one of the seven-storey tall masts and Reinhard, in boyish mood, had daringly climbed to the top of it. The 13 masts and most of the steelwork was fabricated by the end of the year, leaving only the welding to be done. More of the material had arrived from the US and the arduous task of glueing the computer-patterned panels together was beginning. A pressing need as the tent crew entered 1982 was the five kilometres of steel cable, which alone was going to cost about R180 000. The rest of the fabric was also expected in 1982 and payment, of course, would also have to be made. By the grace of God the accounts were being met as Christians gave unqualified support to this captivating mission project.

The project, because of its unique character and because the work was being done by a relatively small crew, was taking much longer than expected, and inflation was also pushing costs higher and higher, putting a lot of stress on the finances which all the while had to sustain the normal crusade expenditure and the upkeep and transport of the existing yellow tent. However, the Big Tent was becoming more and more of a reality and the vision of this mighty "harvester" was steadily percolating among Christians around the world. All who heard Reinhard speak about the project were waiting and praying for the great day when the Big Tent would open its flaps to let in a flood of precious African souls.

Zambia is still very much upon Reinhard's heart and there is no doubt that when the Big Tent starts rolling north, Zambia will be one of the early stops.

A letter arrived at the Witfield offices one day from a young man who was saved during the meetings in Kitwe. His closing paragraph was really touching. It read: "Please come back soon so that we can shame the devil with that new tent of yours."

In December 1982, some of the CFAN staff went to Botswana and Zambia on holiday. They were amazed to see the evidence of those earlier CFAN crusades still alive in the community.

Gabi Wentland, wife of present tentmaster Winfried Wentland, wrote this report which appeared in the ministry magazine, "Revival Report":

"I was at the mighty tent crusades held in Zambia from July to November 1981. During those meetings I saw multitudes of people blessed and thousands accept Jesus Christ as their personal Saviour.

"The question in my heart as we left for Zambia for a short holiday 18 months later was: will we see any results of those crusades?

"Well, when we arrived at the border post I was thrilled when a soldier pricked up his ears when he heard the name CFAN. 'We haven't forgotten your meetings in our country,' he said, and we were warmly welcomed. And then, as we sped along the winding road from Livingstone to Lusaka, we saw more 'signs' of the CFAN influence.

"Alongside the road I spotted children playing and wearing yellow T-shirts and written on them were "Christ for All Nations" and "I belong to Jesus".

" When we arrived in the capital of Lusaka we

discovered that many local church choirs had been named after Pastor Bonnke. And singing with all their hearts these choirs still voice the songs they learnt in the tent meetings. It thrilled my soul.

"What a joy it was to hear testimonies from those many people who had found Christ in the meetings. One White nursing sister told us of the wonderful change that come over the lives of her two servants. 'They are real Christians now,' she exclaimed.

"A young Sunday school teacher repeats the children's lessons over and over again to the kids in her church and teaches them the songs she learnt during the crusade.

"One young soldier stopped us at a road block near Ndola and asked us for our destination. When he saw the yellow CFAN T-shirt my husband Winfried was wearing, he quickly asked: 'Are you the CFAN team?' When we told him we were he recalled how he had been on duty outside our tent during a meeting and when the altar call was made he was saved. 'I stopped smoking and drinking from that day. Later I was filled with the Holy Spirit and now I worship regularly at a nearby church.' He blessed us as we drove off, heading further north.

"At a petrol station a young minister noticed us and begged us to return for another crusade. 'When you left our country it felt as though we went to a funeral,' he said trying to express his desire to see the wonderful saving power of God manifest again in Zambia."

For those who are critical of mass evangelism that report surely must refute the argument that the big crusade does not bear lasting fruit.

# CHAPTER 23

## Walking a cash tightrope

When it comes to his work Reinhard possesses the explosive energy of a sprinter as well as the endurance of a long distance runner. The workload that he is prepared to bear increases each year and 1982 was no exception.

It started off with an eye-opening visit to Zaire. With the prospect of the tent coming on stream at long last, he felt it important to increase contacts in neighbouring African countries. His experience on arrival in Kinsasha, capital of Zaire, was hair-raising. His plane touched down late at night and after clearing customs he caught a taxi, giving the driver the address to where he was to be taken.

They had gone only a short distance when the taxi stopped and two men jumped in and sat in the back. Reinhard, sensing that the men were probably robbers, began to pray under his breath. Then followed a harrowing drive through dark, back streets of Kinsasha which lasted an incredible four hours. He later learnt that the trip should not have taken more than 20 minutes! Nothing happened to Reinhard. His two mystery companions in the back eventually left and Reinhard believes that it was the providence of God that cared for him during the strange taxi ride. He had no suitcase with him because it had been lost at the air terminal in Paris and it was probably his lack of luggage that saved him from being mugged and robbed.

The next day Reinhard met with several church leaders and one man in particular caught his attention – a man known to most Pentecostal Christians simply as Brother Alexander. Zaire, because of its colonization by the Belgians historically has a strong Roman Catholic background, but today there is a powerful, vibrant evangelical witness sweeping through the country. He found that in Kinsasha, alone, there were 82 Pentecostal churches and that the growth rate of the movement was phenomenal, with over 2 500 new churches having sprung up in the past seven years.

Brother Alexander has been a key figure in the amazing Holy Ghost revival in Zaire, which in some aspects bears similarities with the Indonesian revival described by Mel Tari in his book "Like a Mighty Wind". Reinhard found that the outstanding feature of the revival was the simplicity of the faith of the people, who found no difficulty in believing and expecting for even the most impossible miracles. That, in fact, was how the great awakening had begun.

Brother Alexander, a man with a very elementary education, started to pray for the sick and people were miraculously healed. One day some people brought a corpse in the middle of a meeting that Brother Alexander was conducting. It was the body of a young woman and next to it stood a young man, the fiancè, who defiantly threw out a challenge. "You say God raises people from the dead. Here is a test for you".

The woman had already been dead for four days and the stench in the small, stuffy room was almost unbearable, according to Brother Alexander. But he called the little congregation together around the corpse and they lifted up their hands and began to praise and rejoice for about 20 minutes. Suddenly Brother Alexander felt somebody tug his jacket and when he opened his eyes he saw that the corpse was missing. He looked around and saw the "dead" woman standing among those who were praying, eyes closed, hands up, praising God.

When the rest of the congregation saw her they bolted out of the door with Brother Alexander in hot pursuit. The miracle shook the whole area and people turned to God in huge numbers. When relating this amazing story Reinhard makes the pointed comment that missionaries, with all their training and sophistication had failed to achieve in a hundred years, what was now being accomplished by an indigenous man who preached a simple gospel message and who believed that Jesus is alive today to perform the same miracles that He did on the shores of Galilee.

This amazing account of the corpse returning to life may be hard for some to believe, especially when viewed against the patchwork of tribal cultures and lack of any substantial medical reports, but Reinhard had no doubts in his heart after meeting and staying with a married couple in Kinsasha, who told him a truly amazing story, which again involved Brother Alexander, and which was readily confirmed by medical experts.

The husband was a top government official and his wife the manager of a bank in Kinsasha. They were a sophisticated, well educated couple and financially well off. But their marriage was on the point of breaking up because the wife could not have children.

She had visited specialists in Belgium and America and because of certain internal disorders she had eventually been forced to have a hysterectomy and she was left with only half an ovary. The chances of bearing any children were very remote.

One day while the couple were walking in the street in Kinsasha a man had come up to them — it was Brother Alexander. He told the couple: "In the name of Jesus Christ if you are willing to surrender your lives to the Lord, this is what God is going to do for you: you are going to give birth to four children. The first child will be a girl and her name shall be Daisey, the second will be a boy, named Samuel . . ."

At this point the story was interrupted, recalls Reinhard, when a door opened and a little girl came into the room.

"Pastor Bonnke, here comes Daisey" said the mother with tears in her eyes.

"As I stared, I saw behind the little girl a toddler, just learning to balance," said Reinhard.

"And here comes Samuel . . . and I am waiting for Number Three," smiled the mother.

"I was really touched by that testimony. Truly, all things are possible with God," says Reinhard.

During his short stay Reinhard preached at one service attended by 1 500 people. Those who couldn't get inside the hall stood outside on the street, trying desperately to catch a few words from the service inside. "The people were hungry for the Word of God. They came with pencil and paper taking down everything I said. The hall was so packed that it was impossible for me to move around to pray for anybody. I asked those who needed healing to lay their hands on themselves and when I prayed I sensed a surge of the power of God which I had never experienced before anywhere. Immediately crutches were tossed in the air and people began to testify. It was a rain of miracles!" recalled Reinhard.

From Zaire he flew back to Johannesburg to prepare for the first crusade of 1982, which was scheduled for Madadeni, Newcastle, in Natal. It got the year off to a thrilling start with over 6 000 people recording decisions for the Lord in the two-weeks that the crusade lasted. Sharing the tent meetings with Reinhard was Pastor Kenneth Meshoe, who had joined CFAN some years earlier specifically to oversee the youth work. Over the years he had matured as a fine speaker, able to hold his own in front of all audiences. Preaching to a tent full of people Reinhard couldn't help remember the first time he had held a meeting in Newcastle. That had been 15 years earlier just before he'd left to take up his post in Lesotho and on that occasion his audience had been but a handful. Indeed, a lot had happened during those 15 years.

Besides the nightly tent meetings a missions breakfast was held in a local hotel and two open air rallies staged in the nearby sports stadium. At the final Sunday afternoon rally there was an outstanding healing, witnessed by hundreds of people. A local woman got out of her wheelchair and walked. She had suffered from cancer of the pelvis for four years and had slowly become crippled until she had been forced to use a wheelchair. When hands were laid on her she rose to her feet and walked, pushing her wheelchair in front of her up the grassy slope of the stadium to her parked motor car, while hundreds of people stood gaping in unbelief.

The pace of the Newcastle crusade was maintained during April when the famous yellow tent was pitched in Pietermaritzburg and decisions for the Lord topped 8 000. A rally was also held at the Jan Smuts stadium where Whites, Indians, Coloureds and Blacks joined together in spiritual unity to praise and worship God.

The Pietermaritzburg crusade also produced another wheelchair miracle. Mr Gordon Everton of Pietermaritzburg, who had been disabled for 27 years and restricted to a wheelchair for the past year, got to his feet after being prayed for by Pastor Kolisang. Mr Everton said later on that he felt so well that he was considering returning to his work as a welder.

Reinhard's interpreter at this crusade was Pastor Vilakazi, who had the misfortune to have his house broken into and all his clothing stolen. A few days before the crusade ended Pastor Vilakazi arrived home to find all his stolen clothing lying on his bed, drycleaned and neatly folded with a note pinned to them. It read: "I'm sorry for having stolen your clothes. Three days ago I accepted the Lord Jesus in your big yellow tent. Please forgive me."

Although it is the miraculous that often draws the crowd, it is these testimonies which give Reinhard greatest satisfaction. He's a convinced believer in healing being a part of the atonement and he constantly prays for the sick "but to me the greatest miracle on earth is when a person is born into the family of God", says Reinhard. It is this life-changing gospel which he proclaims, that propels him on his great adventure to win Africa for Jesus.

Early in 1982 Rev Paul Yonggi Chou, pastor of the world famous Central Full Gospel Church in Seoul, South Korea, invited Reinhard to visit his church. He was excited to receive the invitation and admits that during his stay with Yonggi Chou he had a thousand questions for the man who has the world's biggest church.

"I could hardly believe my own eyes. Yonggi told me that the church was growing at the rate of 9 000 people a month. At the Sunday service I could not believe my eyes − it was like an anthill, starting at six o'clock in the morning thousands of people flocking in to hear the Word of God, then going out to be replaced by another bunch. I was told that the Church is growing four times faster than the natural population increase and that if the momentum is continued − and I'm sure it will − then by 1990 fifty per cent of the population will be Christian."

The time spent with Yonggi Chou and the visible evidence of the huge numbers, was another great tonic for Reinhard. It gave him the reassurance that even a man like him needs, from time to time, the reassurance that his vision, "Africa shall be saved" was not going to become a hollow-sounding slogan that would echo on like a commercial. "When I saw what he was doing and how the Lord was blessing him I said: 'Lord, I've trusted you for peanuts.'"

He returned to South Africa with his faith level running high − and just as well, because although the Big Tent was now nearing its final stages, a giant cash problem was on the way. More of the material was needed for the completion of the panels, but the order could not be shipped out until payment was made.

The final payment due was R150 000 and there was the possibility of the suppliers cancelling the whole contract, which meant a potential loss of the R350 000 already paid. A deadline for the payment was set by the American company and Reinhard and the CFAN team prayed harder and harder as their faith was forced to walk on the edge of a precipice with a yawning valley of disaster waiting to swallow the whole project.

A little money came in and Reinhard's secretary, Susan Pfister, eagerly waited for the post each day, expecting that the money would surely arrive through the post. But nothing came. The deadline drew nearer and if it had been possible to look into the spirit world and see how Reinhard's shield of faith was standing up it would have probably been battered and buckled and far from the gleaming symbol with which he started off a few years ago.

It was an anxious period, but Reinhard drew strength from the fact that the Big Tent was not his project. "I never sat down and schemed it all out. This is God's tent" and so he waited for "deliverance" to come.

Then on a Monday morning, with just two days left before the deadline expired, the Bonnke family sat down at the breakfast table. While at the table the telephone rang and Reinhard answered it. It was a long distance call from Germany, from a man whom Reinhard had never met.

The man's agitated voice came over the telephone wire: "Pastor Bonnke I cannot sleep at night . . ."

Reinhard admits that when he heard that opening statement he thought it was someone wanting him to pray for them over the telephone, so he enquired as to what the problem was.

The man continued: "Pastor Bonnke when I close my eyes at night all I see in front of me is your face! and I hear a voice saying: 'Pastor Bonnke urgently needs money.' Is that so?''

Inside Reinhard's breast a symphony of hallelujah's began to echoe as he replied: "Yes, that is so.''

Back came the urgent question. "How much do you need?''

A holy excitement stirred inside Reinhard as he replied as calmly as he could: "I cannot tell you. If I tell you the amount you will think I am being cheeky.''

Back came a despairing plea: "Please Pastor Bonnke tell me. I must know the amount.''

"Well, all right. I need R150 000 right now,'' said Reinhard.

There was a silence, broken only by a crackle across the telephone wires then came a stunning reply: "I will transfer it today.''

Reinhard stood transfixed by what he heard and then erupted into a crescendo of hallelujahs that turned a humble breakfast into a thanksgiving banquet as he and his family rejoiced at this 11th hour deliverance.

The mysterious caller, a Roman Catholic, was true to his promise and the money was duly transferred — and he got a good night's rest!

When recounting this story to audiences around the world, Reinhard impishly adds: "You see, I slept like a baby because I knew the Lord would not let us down. Yet the man who had the money could not sleep!''

It was a spectacular and miraculous financial provision, but one which stretched many of the team's faith to breaking point. But the ministry's "daily bread'' is not always provided in such a startling way. With thousands of faithful prayer partners scattered in many lands, the money often comes in small amounts.

Often in the CFAN mail there is a grubby, grease-stained letter and inside a postal order for 50 cents from some poor widow living in a remote area. When those amounts come in Reinhard is sharply reminded of the widow's mite — and never to despise even the most meagre amount.

The financial aspect of Reinhard's work is, of course, one of the areas which always arouses curiosity, especially among worldly-minded people. When the Big Tent project is mentioned and the millions of Rands involved, people begin to wonder why people are so eager to subscribe to it. Are they just gullible? Of course, those outside of the Church often dismiss the whole thing as one big con trick, and credit Reinhard with using wily psychological ploys and playing on the emotions of people to donate. But Reinhard never pulls hard on the emotional heart strings when it comes to finance.

Instead he plays a gentle lullabye when an appeal for money is made, in contrast to his very strong call to sinners to come forward to the altar. Then he orchestrates a full symphony on the heart strings of the sinner. He makes no apologies for a powerful emotional call when he's finished preaching the gospel. Then he trusts the Holy Spirit to tug the hearts of the repentant and when he's making a gentle appeal for money he also trusts the Holy Spirit to do the tugging — this time on the wallets.

It is true to say that he has no formula for his financial support, except of course, that he does trust God to provide for all of his needs. It is also true that he does have a way of getting people to respond, without them even being aware of it. One pastor explained it this way: "When I hear Bonnke preach my hand is itching to give. But when I hear other men preach I often feel like going up to them and asking for a credit!"

After the cash crisis with the Big Tent the hard-working crew took a deep breath as they ploughed on. The steel masts were almost all completed, the steel cable and the giant shackles were on hand and the massive anchor equipment was also taking shape. When the material arrived from America the back-breaking job of cutting and then glueing began. Every part of the project was BIG − except the work force, who laboured long, long hours trying to make up time. And at last the engineers were able to make a firm, calculated prediction for the first test erection − November/December.

Reinhard had, of course, been continually predicting dates for the erection, ever since the project first started and now at last he knew that he would be able to have some solid proof for the people to see. All this time he had been conscious of the fact that even some of his dearest prayer partners were beginning to doubt the wisdom of the Big Tent and he realised that the tent had to go up as soon as possible. Three years had passed since the first plans were drawn in 1979.

The other disturbing factor was, of course, the cost of the project. Although the actual cost of the structure of the tent was still within the R1,5-million budget, the additional equipment and transport which would be needed to make the giant mobile cathedral functional had rocketed the eventual cost to R4,5-million, allowing for the ravages of inflation. Despite the serious mounting costs, Reinhard who if he had not been called into the ministry, would have most certainly become an entrepreneur, decided to expand his headquarters and the property adjoining their land was purchased for R215 000. On it was a large house, which was to be extended to provide accommodation for the extra fulltime staff and also provide a depot for the transport fleet which would be needed for the Big Tent.

By mid-1982 Reinhard was a happy man. He had been in Germany for the month of May and had returned to embark on a return crusade to Swaziland, which was spiced by a special guest in the person of the American astronaut Charles Duke of the Apollo 16 mission, who was touring southern Africa sharing his testimony at specially arranged meetings.

# CHAPTER 24

## The masts go up!

The Swaziland crusade took the now familiar pattern and was given an added boost with many members of the royal house of Swaziland attending some of the meetings. For Reinhard the year thundered on with more and more preaching engagements. An ever increasing demand was being made on him to attend mission breakfasts and banquets. These proved ideal to promote and share the vision in the smaller, rural towns and by this means hundreds more were added to his prayer partner list.

After Swaziland came further tent crusades at Thlbani, Rustenburg, Ga-Rankuwa, Mabopane and Hammanskraal. Laced in between these was a visit to the University of Zululand at Empangeni, a weekend rally in Ladysmith, a flying visit to Nairobi to attend the World Pentecostal Conference, another brief campaign in Germany in October, a CFAN prayer partners conference at home base and a weekend rally in Cape Town.

In between all of this were the breakfast and dinner engagements as well as invitations from various churches throughout the country. His life was becoming one of perpetual motion, jetting from one centre to the next to preach the gospel he loves so much.

Massive crowds continued to fill the yellow tent at each crusade venue and the rallies, held in sports arenas, like the Greenpoint stadium, in Cape Town, were almost filled. As always each meeting spawned a dozen or more touching stories and the pace of the campaigns became so hectic that it was difficult for Betty Lore, CFAN's fulltime reporter, to keep up with the testimonies that flowed from the crusades.

An unusual story from the Rustenburg crusade involved the case of the till dipper and the furniture thief.

A husband and wife came to see some of the CFAN pastors after one of the meetings and explained their predicament. The wife was saved in the tent meetings and now she wanted to confess that she had been taking money out of the till at the shop where she had previously worked. She had a burning desire in her heart to make matters right since Jesus had cleansed her of all past sin.

Her husband, who had been a backslider, had returned to the Lord. He worked in a trusted position at a local furniture store and confessed that his home was furnished with goods stolen from the shop. He, too, wanted to put matters right. The prospects for the couple certainly didn't look bright. In fact, it looked as though a jail sentence was awaiting them. But they were determined to face their employers. So they went off, accompanied by two CFAN pastors.

They first went to the wife's former employer. He listened to the story and when they had finished he told them he, himself, was a born again Christian. He reasoned that if the woman had confessed to God her sin and she was now forgiven he was obliged to do the same. He refrained from penalising her in any way.

The group then went to the furniture store. The manager agreed to keep on the man, on condition that he paid for all the stolen furniture. But a day later the general manager of the furniture shop heard about the incident. He called in the man and told him he could keep the furniture and need not pay for it!

It's stories like these that underline the scripture, "old things pass away and all things become new". Like the story of Jerry "Lucky" Selekane. Jerry described himself as a "fully fledged child of the devil" – before he met Jesus. He was one of the thousands who came to the Mabopane crusade, near Pretoria.

His surrender to Jesus caused quite a stir in the district because he was so well known. He had terrorized people, mugging them and threatening them with an evil-looking knife. In fact, Jerry was not afraid to use that knife and three years previously he had stabbed his best friend in the back, leaving him paralysed and confined to a wheelchair. Jerry served six months in jail on a manslaughter charge.

On his release from prison he heard that relatives of the stabbed man had sworn revenge on him. Jerry went into hiding at an aunt's hut and while there he suffered a stroke and became semi-paralysed. He went to the local witchdoctor for help, but grew steadily worse. He suffered from sudden and severe convulsions and during one of these seizures he lapsed into a coma. "I dreamed I was dying and when I woke up I found my aunt and uncle at my bedside holding my hand."

It was with this background that Jerry came to the yellow tent. He knew this was his last chance in life. Even before the preaching started Jerry gave his life to the Lord as he was warmed in his heart while listening to the voices of the huge congregation singing and praising God.

It was one thing to give your life to the Lord, but now Jerry had to face up to the realities of his position and that meant facing up to the people who had sworn revenge. The CFAN pastors urged him to go back to his best friend and try to make restitution. At first he resisted for fear of the relatives, but when the CFAN workers said they would go with him, he agreed.

Too afraid even to show himself, he waited in hiding while the CFAN pastors went inside the house. The paralysed man said he was willing to forgive Jerry, but the mother and the rest of the family refused. They wanted revenge. So to avoid any ugly incidents Jerry and the pastors left. Jerry continued to come to the meetings each night, rejoicing in his salvation.

He became so bold and confident in his new-found faith that he made an unconditional and courageous decision: "I'm going to face the family," he told the pastors, "even if they shoot me." So the next morning Jerry and some of the team went to see the paralysed man and his family. The atmosphere was tense, but after much earnest talking the mother agreed to forgive the man who had stabbed her son. Jerry freely offered to repay the money she had spent on buying a wheelchair for her son.

A couple of months later Jerry made a special trip to attend a CFAN prayer partner conference at Witfield, and he was still ablaze with the love of God. He had truly come to know the love of God, not to only to save his own soul, but to bring reconciliation and peace among those whom he had hurt and who had vowed to hunt him down like a dog and kill him.

Several volumes would have been needed to describe the hundreds of tales of changed lives, deliverance from evil, and physical healing that occurred during 1982 and each one was very precious to Reinhard, but when he looks back on that year only one event is clearly etched into his mind — the Big Tent. For at last he saw it standing and after four years he would at last be able to tell his faithful supporters that it was a reality.

Right from the day, back in 1979, when the first sketch was made, Reinhard had been unflagging in his zeal and determination to see the project carried through to the end. Men of lesser calibre would have folded and shelved what at times looked like an impossible dream. Even the men who worked on the project had to admit that there were several occasions during the four years that they doubted whether it was really feasible. But like Gideon's brave band they stuck manfully to their task and as the lift-off day approached they, too, began to heave a sigh of relief that their labours had not been in vain.

CFAN's general manager Peter Vandenberg negotiated to lease a large piece of land opposite a hyperstore at Boksburg and the tent crew began the arduous job of ferrying the steel masts, the kilometres of steel cable, the truck loads of shackles, bolts and chains, the massive main anchors and, of course, the precious roof material, from Springs, 35 km away, to the test site. It was decided to only raise six of the 13 masts for the test run.

Drilling began for the anchors and the test site proved a good location because half of the ground was made up of a soft, clay composition and on the northern extreme of the site, the drillers hit solid rock. Once the anchors had been secured — and some hitches ironed out — the next big job was the raising of the six masts. Six giant mobile cranes trundled onto the site, which began to take on the appearance of a wharfside quay and at the end of the day there was a huge cheer as all six of the seven-storey tall masts stood proudly pointing heavenward.

Reinhard is not a man to cry easily, but he did that day. He had been away on business during the day and did not know that the masts were up. He was driving home along the freeway when something new and unfamiliar caught his vision. He looked again, and then it dawned on him that he was looking at the Big Tent masts. "My soul was flooded with happiness and tears rolled down my cheeks as I thanked God from the bottom of my heart for this miracle."

A lot of old fashioned sweat and muscle went into the strenuous job of "pumping" up the fabric. But every stroke of the hydraulic jack was happily endured as the fabric inched skyward. Some difficulties were encountered on one of the masts, but by nightfall the fabric was waving gently in the breeze and all that had to be done the next day was to tighten up and tension the cables.

But during that Friday night a tremendous thunder storm, accompanied by high winds and hail struck the East Rand and when the crew saw the tent the next morning tons of water was trapped in the tent, which now had a comical inverted appearance. Damage, though, was slight and the tent crew had learnt a big lesson. Further technical hitches were experienced on a section of the tent which had been designed for the platform and pulpit area. After much hair-pulling the boffins agreed to dispense with this section, which would in fact do away with the 13th mast.

Meanwhile, all this activity had caught the attention of the local newspapers and even in Durban, the "Sunday Tribune" ran a full page story on the Big Tent, which was headlined SEVENTH-STOREY HEAVEN. More and more people were taking notice of this massive project and a technical journal in Britain also enquired about the structure which was being hailed — and quite correctly — as a "world first".

As the year closed, Reinhard and his team took a well earned break and after four years the vision was a reality. The tent, albeit only a section of it, stood proudly next to the main freeway on the East Rand — a symbol firstly to God's supernatural provision of finance and secondly to the faith of an evangelist who was prepared to dare all for Jesus.

The big question now was when would the Big Tent be ready for its first campaign? The engineers still wanted to carry out many more tests, especially those connected with safety margins. Speculation was that the official dedication of the tent would be early in 1983, but from the brief experience gained in moving the masses of equipment from one site to another and also the length of time needed to prepare the site and also time to dismantle, made one thing very obvious to everybody — transport, in quantity, was needed badly. The technicians also realised that they needed at least one more trial run before opening the Big Tent for a full-blooded crusade.

These were some of the tent considerations that were carried into 1983 and as the months slipped by money, as always, continued to be a pressing issue, and linked with it what was now a top priority —

transport. Eighteen giant trucks were required to carry the monster tent and the cost of these, alone, was R1,5-million.

# CHAPTER 25

## Disaster — then triumph

There is no doubt that 1983 was the most hectic year of Reinhard's life and there were some misgivings among those close to him about the wisdom of the pace that he was setting for himself. Internationally he travelled more than 150 000 km and in southern Africa covered at least 50 000 km, preaching at crusades, rallies, churches, banquets and conventions. Reinhard Bonnke, evangelist to Africa, was undoubtedly now recognised as one of the world's leading figures in evangelism. In the past three years his personal ministry had exploded and his crusade organisers, Sam Tshabalala and Mike Eltringham could hardly cope with the invitations.

The year began with a crusade at Mamelodi, Pretoria and as soon as that had concluded, he, Pastor Kolisang and his crusade soloist Tommy Saaiden, were jetting out across the Indian Ocean for a two-night stand in Perth, then on to Auckland, New Zealand to conduct a city-wide campaign.

In Perth, the trio suffered badly from jet-lag and singer Tommy Saaiden nodded off to sleep while Reinhard was preaching. For anybody to doze while Reinhard is holding the floor is quite a feat. In one Perth meeting Reinhard had a quiet chuckle to himself when the Lord gave him a word of knowledge concerning someone with a stiff left arm. He called out to the audience that the Lord desired to heal the stiff arm and the words had hardly passed his lips, when a dear lady in the front row piped up with typical Aussie brashness: "Tell me, pastor, will a right leg do?"

When they arrived in Auckland they found that 26 Pentecostal churches had been preparing since October 1982 for the crusade which was held in the Logan Campbell Centre. Pastor Rob Wheeler, who heads a large independent church in the city, had been the man to initiate the invitation. They were not disappointed as up to 3 000 to 4 000 filled the auditorium each night and the daily newspaper "The Auckland Star" blazed a headline across an inside page: FIERY EVANGELIST 'PLUNDERS HELL TO POPULATE HEAVEN'. The local newspaper carried reports and interviews with people with whom Reinhard had prayed and who had been healed.

The media men also probed Reinhard and his colleagues on their political attitudes concerning South Africa. But none of the CFAN team allowed themselves to be drawn into the arena of politics. Reinhard's answer to the media was a polite and firm: "I am not part of the problem − I am part of the solution. I am an ambassador for Jesus and not for any country."

Returning to South Africa in February he was immediately back on the platform of his dearly loved yellow crusade tent. This crusade, at Dennilton, was marked by a considerable amount of demon manifestation, a reminder once again that the real battle is not against flesh and blood, but against spiritual forces.

During February a small CFAN team held a weekend rally at the Westbourne Stadium in Port Elizabeth. One great moment in the rally was when an elderly lady, Mrs Elizabeth Louw, got up out of her wheelchair after Pastor Kolisang had prayed for her. She suffered from severe rheumatism and arthritis and had been confined to the wheelchair for the past year. It was a crowning moment in the meeting when some of the pastors lifted the wheelchair high into the air to show the crowd the reality of the miracle. The 63-year-old Mrs Louw further demonstrated her healing by pushing the wheelchair out of the stadium. A little six-year-old girl, Princess Jakavula who had been born lame and was forced to wear leg irons had them removed and walked perfectly after being prayed for by Reinhard. These were just two of the many exciting testimonies that came out of this rally.

In March Reinhard was stepping on to another Jumbo jet. This time his destination was America. He had visited there many times previously and had spoken in many churches, but still it seemed as though he could not get the breakthrough he wanted among American Christians.

His wife Anni and crusade singer Tommy Saaiden accompanied him for the month-long preaching tour of the US and when he returned, after stopping off briefly in Brazil, he reported on a satisfactory response. It had been the best that he had ever received and important contacts were made and bridges built for the future. The American connection was, at long last, being tied more securely and it was to pay off handsome dividends at the end of 1983.

When he had left South Africa for America the rest of the CFAN team had been preparing for the next tent crusade, which was to be at a place called Tafelkop, in the Northern Transvaal. While at a meeting in Houston, Texas, Reinhard had received a message from his secretary Susan asking him to contact her urgently. He knew it must be serious and his thoughts immediately jumped to the Big Tent. Was there trouble?

At the first opportunity he telephoned South Africa, waking up his secretary at 3 o'clock in the morning. The news she had was chilling: "The tent has blown down . . . the one at Tafelkop." When Susan had mentioned "tent blown down" he had got an awful sinking feeling, but then he realised it was the old yellow one. But it was almost as serious because for the present this was his only workable crusade tent. Without it his crusade work would be in serious trouble.

He spent an anxious night in prayer, not knowing the extent of the damage. The details that Susan had been able to give him were still sketchy. All he knew was that there had been a storm and the masts had collapsed bringing everything down on the congregation of about 3 000 people. To the best of her knowledge nobody had been seriously injured.

On his arrival from Brazil he learnt the full story. The crusade proper had come to an end and the follow-up team were conducting nightly teaching classes for the new converts.

Early one evening as the new Christians filled up the wooden benches nearest to the platform, eager to learn more about the things of God a fierce wind had suddenly come up. When the first gusts had struck the tent, the crew had immediately leapt into action to let down the side walls and tighten up the ropes. But they could not contend with the speed and the ferocity of the wind, which from all accounts seems to have been a tornado, although these are extremely rare in this part of the country.

Suzette Hattingh, head of CFAN's women's ministry, who was on the platform at the time gave this vivid description of what happened next:

"The wind hit the tent and then it seemed to blow up like a balloon, then deflate. It inflated a second time and then everything seemed to come loose. The main iron beam running across the centre of the tent lifted. Poles lifted and everything began to rattle and fall. It was like watching a tidal wave in slow motion. Only this tidal wave was a mass of yellow canvas, cables, lights and poles.

"I have never seen so many people move so quickly to get out of a tent. I'm sure the angels must have helped them get out. A mast at the back of the tent twisted and collapsed and the one above the platform where I was standing began to bend like a bow. I remember our organist doing a somersault over the edge of the platform and disappearing into the night. I mention that because moments later I found myself almost alone in the tent and in the background an automatic, melodic beat — it was the organ."

Richard Walters, an American with CFAN and who is in charge of the follow-up work, was trapped under the sea of canvas for a while, but escaped unhurt. There was hardly any hysteria, despite the fact that many mothers had lost their children in the wild exodus from the tent. When the CFAN team visited the site the following day they were amazed at the destruction caused by the wind and even more amazed at how God had miraculously protected the more than 3 000 people who had been inside the tent when the wind struck.

The destruction of the yellow tent looked like causing the postponement of the following crusade which was scheduled for a place called Syabuswa, which is in the Marble Hall area. It was planned to begin in April and had already been advertised. Insurers, meanwhile were called in to assess the damage, and it was estimated that the tent would be out of commission for at least two months while the shredded canvas was fixed. The immediate question, though, was whether to cancel the Syabuswa crusade or to go ahead and hold it in the open air. Remembering his past experiences of open air meetings made him hesitate before he made the decision: the crusade goes on.

Being in April the weather was still warm at night and the only deterent would be rain. The length of the crusade was shortened to only one week, but what a week it was. The site for the meeting was situated about a half a kilometer away from the Syabuswa post office on an open piece of bushland. The platform, which had survived the Tafelkop tornado was placed in position and two of the servicable masts from the yellow tent were erected to carry the floodlights and speakers. The normal crusade benches were laid out under the hot sun and Reinhard and the team waited to see what would happen.

Then, as the sun slid away in a fiery blaze of red and rosy pink, the long files of people began to appear from all parts of the district and the shadowy figures in the night suddenly became a mass of people almost 6 000-strong. Night after night the crowds rolled in, until on the final Saturday night almost 12 000 people gathered under a cloudless, starry sky to meet with the

God who hangs the universe on the enduring and faithful power of His Word. The people of Syabuswa were richly blessed and thousands gave their hearts to the Lord during this shortened crusade.

The popularity of Reinhard and the CFAN crusade team can be gauged from this amusing anecdote told by a lecturer at the local college. "I was speaking to my religious instruction class on the Second Coming of the Lord and while discussing the subject I had interjected a question to the class, 'Tell me what great event are we waiting for?' Without hesitation back came the answer, 'The arrival of Pastor Bonnke and the CFAN team!'"

Just when the staff at the Witfield base were getting used to seeing Reinhard around the offices, he drove off to Jan Smuts airport. This time his destination was Helsinki, Finland. But before he arrived there he stopped off in Copenhagen, Denmark for two reasons: to preach in one of the city's big Pentecostal churches and to fulfill a radio interview for a Christian station in Adelaide, Australia.

News of Reinhard and his Big Tent had started to filter through Australia and one of that country's major Christian magazines, "Australia's New Day" had featured a lengthy article which had been subtitled: REINHARD BONNKE: AFRICA'S BILLY GRAHAM. The editor of the magazine Barry Chant had been so excited by the story and the vision of the Big Tent that he had contacted CFAN's headquarters so as to arrange a telephone interview. Because of his tight schedule the only way the interview could be done was for the Australians to phone him in Copenhagen. The link-up was achieved and Reinhard was able to tell thousands more about his vision for a "bloodwashed Africa". God was providing new ways and new opportunities at every turn for the promotion of this great mission. This, of course, is why Reinhard pushed himself on relentlessly throughout 1983. He just did not want to miss any open door and those that were only slightly ajar he was going to burst open.

When he arrived in Helsinki he thought he was a candidate for a general election because everywhere he looked he could see only REINHARD BONNKE. His name was plastered everywhere and as he stood on the pavement outside his hotel he even saw his name and photograph going past him on the side of a tram car. Huge billboard photographs peered down at him in the market square. The Finnish pastors had worked tirelessly in preparing for the main crusade which was scheduled for an indoor ice stadium in Helsinki with smaller meetings in Pori and Kuopio. Never in all his ministry had he seen such wide publicity, which included a "March for Jesus" through the main streets of Helsinki. In fact, a newspaper had run a poll, which revealed that five per cent of the city's population knew who Reinhard Bonnke was — he was truly amazed.

All the publicity about the visiting German evangelist naturally stirred up the interest of the press, radio and television media. They turned out in force on the opening night of the Helsinki crusade to see who this man was and why he was so popular. They were obviously impressed because when Reinhard returned to his hotel room later that night he flipped on the television set and there he was preaching in the ice stadium.

The next day Helsinki's major afternoon newspaper not only had his picture on the front page, but carried the meeting as the newspaper's main news item of the day. It was headlined: SIGNS AND WONDERS TODAY. The coverage was outstanding and the stadium filled to its capacity of 10 000 people.

The visit proved a new experience in one way. Reinhard's preaching style is one of action, his voice roaring and thundering, then suddenly dropping to a soothing whisper and, of course, heavily punctuated with "hallelujahs" and exclamations of "praise God, praise God". His style invokes hearers to respond with liberal "amens" and echoes of his own "hallelujahs". But when he started preaching in Helsinki his exclamations of praise brought no response, except for a muted "amen" or two from those close to the platform.

But as he preached he noticed women fidgeting in their handbags and men pulling handkerchiefs from pockets and dabbing away tears that rolled down their cheeks. Unlike the more hot-blooded saints in the southern hemisphere the Finns are cool when it comes to expressing religious fervour. Mind you, by the time Reinhard left Finland his infectious preaching had thawed out the Finnish emotions and "hallelujahs" were filling the halls where he spoke.

One night he had the audience in the ice stadium cheering when the Lord touched a gypsy woman who had come forward on a pair of crutches. When he prayed for her she fell to the floor under an anointing of Holy Spirit power. Reinhard told some of the ushers that she would walk once she recovered. A short while later she was helped to her feet, but clung on to her crutches, until Reinhard gently said: "Give them to me."

As she looked in his soft, blue eyes, she saw only the

compassion of Jesus and handed them over and then, with 10 000 pairs of eyes silently watching, the gypsy lady took a few hesitant steps. Then she shouted and began to jump and run and there was pandemonium in the stadium as the Finns forgot their inhibitions.

Night after night the crowds thronged forward to give their hearts to Jesus and long rows of people lined up for prayer. The lines became so long that Reinhard had the people arranged in two rows with a centre pathway and, starting from one end, he walked between them laying hands on the people, two at a time. Once he looked behind him to see everybody lying on the ground and he quipped later: "I looked behind me and thought I had opened the Red Sea!" One night an elderly woman came out for prayer and as he approached her he was suddenly struck by her amazing likeness to his late mother. Bending forward he mentioned the likeness to her and gave her a spontaneous hug and kissed her cheek.

The crowds became so dense that a "bodyguard" was assigned to help get him through the crowds and out the entrance each night and once, while pushing and struggling to get through the pressing throng, Reinhard felt a tug on his jacket. He turned just in time to see a man, desperate to touch him and to ask for prayer, fall to the ground under the power of God. It was a most unusual incident and reminded him of the woman in the Bible, who had lunged out to touch the hem of the Lord's garment.

At another venue newspaper reporters had insisted on a brief interview just before he was due to preach. One woman reporter asked him to pray for her. He did and she crumpled to the floor under the power of God — surely the most unusual way to end a press interview.

He made a sensational hit with the secular press. A popular secular magazine carried huge pictures and a report on the crusades and one reporter, obviously impressed with his oratory, suggested in his column that the members of the Finnish parliament go and hear Reinhard speak. The news of his visit reached as far as Lapland and a group of Christians travelled over 1 000 km to attend some of his meetings.

There was no doubt in Reinhard's heart as he peered out of the airplane porthole at the scenic beauty of the land of a thousands lakes, that the blessing of God had been poured out in a wonderful way. Now, it was back to the land of his calling – Africa.

His next major crusade was in sharp contrast to the Finnish conditions. The yellow tent, now repaired, was pitched in Gaborone, Botswana, which was in the grip of a torturous drought. From the crystal clear atmosphere of Finland he was now sitting in a caravan under the searing African sun with palls of red dust everywhere. But it was a welcome return to the city where his crusade ministry had been launched in 1975.

# CHAPTER 26

## Big Tent trial

The crusade, held in June and July, was a great success. It started with two weeks in Gaborone and then the tent was moved for a two-week spell in Francistown. The crusades realised some happy reunions with those who still recalled the thrilling campaign of 1975, which had launched Reinhard and CFAN on the crusade trail. Among those was Rev W. Scheffers, chairman of the Evangelical Fellowship of Botswana. Recalling that 1975 visit he said: "It was the first time we had seen the power of God demonstrated. Blind eyes opened and cripples walk. Gaborone has not been the same since then."

Another who joyfully renewed his friendship with the CFAN team was Mr Jimmy Sekake, who had been the caretaker at the city hall when Reinhard had hired it for the first meetings in the town. He was saved during those meetings and he and his wife and children are still faithfully serving the Lord today.

The second leg, at Francistown, was even better. After the first night the report was: the blind see! The second night it was: cripples walk! and the news spread rapidly that miracles were happening in the yellow tent and by the end of the two weeks over 5 000 people registered decisions for Jesus.

Reinhard's interpreter at Francistown was Rev Johannes Kgawarapi. In 1975 Reinhard had received a word of knowledge from the Lord that he should look out for a man named "Johannes" at the meeting in the city hall. One of the first people to respond to the altar call that night was "Johannes", who later went to Bible school in Lesotho, then after a year went to Francistown to pastor a church. He completed his Bible course by correspondence and is still pastoring the same church.

The team also met a White farmer who was one of the many volunteer counsellors for the Francistown crusade. He had been saved in Livingstone, Zambia, in 1981 when Reinhard had preached there and he was now working in Botswana, helping to establish a new church as well as leading an outreach to prisoners.

During June and July there were two small incidents which are worth recording for the simple reason that they demonstrate that despite his bubbling faith and seemingly endless energy Reinhard is, after all, still susceptible to the frailities that are common to mankind.

In June he accepted an invitation to preach at Ray McCauley's Rhema church in Randburg as part of a three-day seminar on healing. Reinhard arrived back at Witfield from Gaborone the day before and he was fit for only one place – bed. He and several other members of the CFAN team had picked up a severe 'flu bug in Botswana. It was touch and go whether Reinhard would make the healing seminar, but with family, friends and colleagues earnestly interceding the prayers of the righteous prevailed and he took the podium in the Randburg church.

While the tent was being shifted from Gaborone to

Francistown, Reinhard and a small team headed for balmy Durban for a three-day preaching blitz. The Westridge Park tennis stadium, the Sugar Bowl, was hired for the Friday night, a missions breakfast at a city hotel was scheduled for Saturday morning, then a meeting at a sports stadium in KwaMashu in the afternoon, followed by an open air meeting in the Indian suburb of Chatsworth. On Sunday he was booked to preach at two different churches — one in the morning and at another in the evening.

The Sugar Bowl was crammed on the Friday night and the service saw one victory after another. A 17-year-old youth, Robin Martin, of Windermere Durban, came to the meeting on crutches, but left with them under his arm. This was his testimony: "Three weeks before the rally I tore all the ligaments around my knee while playing rugby. The pain was so terrible and the injury so serious that doctors considered removing the cartilage from the kneecap. When Pastor Bonnke called the people who wanted to be healed to receive Jesus as their Healer, I walked forward painfully on the crutches and stood among the crowd.

"When the prayer started I lifted my arms. My crutches fell to the ground. It felt as though an electric shock had gone through me. The pain in my leg disappeared and I knew I was healed."

Young Robin pushed his way through the crowd and climbed up onto the platform to give immediate testimony to the power and mercy of God and a photographer captured a dramatic picture of the youngster raising his hands in praise and Reinhard waving the crutches in the air.

The meeting ended late and Reinhard had to be up

early next morning for the missions breakfast. He realised then that he would never last the pace for the next two days. So he cancelled the one Sunday meeting, despite the fact that the local pastor had already advertised Reinhard as the guest speaker.

Fortunately the minister was most understanding and Reinhard promised to make it up later in the year, which he did do in October. The KwaMashu meeting started without Reinhard — the lack of sleep had caught up with him and a cat nap turned into a beauty sleep. But he did arrive in time to preach and the altar call saw virtually the whole grandstand full of people come forward to receive Christ.

Rain began falling during the afternoon meeting and the prospects for the Chartsworth rally looked bleak. Rain continued to fall while the wooden benches were laid out, but despite the persistent drizzle many people arrived for the meeting. At 7 o'clock when the meeting was due to get underway the rain ceased and the moon came out. By the time Reinhard came to preach there were 4 000 people gathered in the football field. He was so touched by the openess of the predominantly Hindu-believing Indians that he determined to hold a full scale crusade in one of the Indian areas in 1984.

When Reinhard boarded the plane at Louis Botha airport he was a tired man and although he knew he was pushing himself to the limit he also knew that he had to keep on going. The vision had to be spread.

While back at Witfield for a brief few days he was able to examine the Big Tent progress. The site chosen at KwaThema, Springs, was next to the main housing district and there were also large, open grounds adjacent to the tent site for plenty of parking. It had been decided to raise nine of the 12 masts for this test crusade and activity at Springs was feverish. The month of August was not an ideal time for a crusade on the highveld because of the bitter winter nights, but the year's schedule made it imperative to run the crusade then. If they did not, then there would be no test crusade before the official opening and Dedication Day, which was to be February 18, 1984.

Although all attention was now focussed on preparations for the Springs crusade, Reinhard was again kissing his wife goodbye and heading for the airport — this time Amsterdam and the Billy Graham Conference on evangelism. Reinhard looked forward to this event with special anticipation, not because he would be given an opportunity to speak, but because he desired to make contact with as many evangelists as possible from Africa and where better than at Amsterdam. His keeness to meet these top men stemmed from certain events that happened during his trip to America in March.

The kernel of an idea began to take root and it involved a new word which was to dominate his thinking for the rest of the year — strategy. Africa was the harvest field he was called to and despite the size and effectiveness of his ministry he realised that he needed more allies in this showdown with the devil. He wanted to meet like-minded men and share his vision with them, gain their confidence and co-operation.

While in Tulsa, Oklahoma, he visited the famous evangelist T. L. Osborn, who is probably better known outside of America as one of the all-time greats in mass evangelism and who had also campaigned in Africa and in Nigeria particularly. He and "TL" spent two hours sharing mutual experiences, hopes and plans for the future. Although he got no decisive answers during his discussions with "TL" he knew that he was getting nearer to the solution. The two men parted in a warm spirit of love and fellowship and just before stepping out of "TL's" office Reinhard asked the great evangelist to pray for him.

To this "TL" replied: "No, my brother, you pray for me."

The American had been impressed with his German-born counterpart and the vastness of his vision for Africa and he recognised that here was no ordinary preacher, but a man with a very clear call and anointing on his ministry.

The plan became clearer when he visited Dallas and spoke at the Christ for the nations Institute. He met with students and many of them were from countries in Africa. He invited them to breakfast at the local Holiday Inn. While they shared and fellowshipped over breakfast Reinhard was impressed with the students' desire to see Africa won for Jesus. An anointing of the Spirit came over them all and to the amazement of the hotel staff the breakfast deteriorated into a praise meeting with Reinhard and the students on their knees.

But out of the meeting with T. L. Osborn and the discussion with the students a plan evolved. He was to host a conference of 600 of Africa's top evangelist in Swaziland in October 1984 and with typical flair the conference was to be known as the "Fire" Conference.

So it was with this conference plan burning in his heart that he arrived in Holland and got busy contacting and meeting preachers from Africa. At one meeting he shared his vision for the Big Tent and, as he often does, exclaimed: "We will travel from Cape Town to Cairo with this Big Tent . . ." and before he could finish an Egyptian evangelist stood up, note book and pen in hand and asked: "Tell me Pastor Bonnke, when will you be in Cairo?"

The Amsterdam conference also gave him his first opportunity to meet Dr Billy Graham, who surprised Reinhard by his knowledge of CFAN's ministry. In fact, he told him that he had received a personal report only recently on Reinhard's meetings in Finland. The men spent a cordial 20 minutes together and Reinhard left, happy to have met the man who has spoken to millions during his years as a crusade evangelist.

Back in South Africa all was set for the Big Tent's first crusade trial. On Sunday, July 31, 1983 Reinhard and the CFAN team travelled through on the ministry bus for a special "in-house" service at the tent. The 100-odd tent crew and office staff shared communion together in a simple service. The group hardly filled the first three rows of the centre block and their voices of praise and worship were lost in the cavernous dome of the tent. "The old CFAN is dead," he told his staff, "we are moving into a new dimension". Indeed they were.

The next night the first crusade meeting was held in the Big Tent and the altar call of several hundred was, as Reinhard termed it, "the first-fruits of a new harvest of souls for Africa". The weather during the first two weeks of August was bitterly cold and obviously kept a lot of people indoors. But despite this the attendance built up from about 3 000 on the first night to an average of 7 000 to 8 000. The fruits of the campaign were exciting with 8 000 people registering decisions for the Lord. Although the crowds had been disappointing, the tent crew were well satisfied with the trial run. It had given them the opportunity to test out sound systems, lighting and check out a dozen other items. When the crusade finished Reinhard and the team were happy. A lot of practical experience had been gained and they were confident now that the Dedication Day and the crusade in Soweto would not only be more streamlined, but would fill the tent.

Of course, the Big Tent was still gobbling up the major portion of CFAN'S finances. Transport was still a priority, but drilling rigs, generators, video equipment and many other pieces of equipment were still needed. But in his usual confident manner Reinhard knew that God would not fail him. "God pays for the things he orders and the Big Tent is not mine it is His," was Reinhard's prognosis. However, Reinhard is not a man who makes idle "faith statements". First and foremost Reinhard is a man of great faith; he is also a man who will quickly show you his works. Much prayer was being made for the urgently needed trucks, and Reinhard seized every opportunity to make people aware of CFAN's great need.

During 1983 valuable links were forged with Christian television networks in America when films were flown over to the US and the networks began to get excited when they saw some extraordinary footage of Reinhard's crusade work. In fact, CBN, the biggest Christian network in America, indicated an eagerness to interview Reinhard. It was clear that new doors were opening and when Barry Hon, a quietly-spoken millionaire from California, met Reinhard during a visit to South Africa and learnt about his ministry, he promised to assist in promoting CFAN in America. Reinhard also initiated a special American edition of his local "Revival Report" and called it "Africa Revival" which was aimed at keeping American prayer partners informed about what was happening in his ministry. The American connection certainly looked like becoming stronger as his work began to gain more international recognition.

# CHAPTER 27

## Trucks for Africa!

Following the KwaThema crusade Reinhard led a small team for a three-day crusade in Kampala, Uganda. When he walked into the immigration area at the Kampala air terminal a warning sign stared him right in the face. Visitors needed certain health certificates and he didn't have them. Muttering a prayer he went to the nearest desk and opened his passport for the official. The man looked up at Reinhard, his face beaming like the sun, as he shouted aloud: "Pastor Bonnke! Praise the Lord!" Needless to say he had no difficulties with any of his documents!

From the moment he arrived Reinhard was struck by the depth of the dedication of the Christians of Kampala. While in the Uganda capital he stayed with a top-ranking government official.

His host had some fascinating and blood-curdling tales to tell about the Idi Amin reign of terror and many of the accounts were first hand because his host had been an official in the Amin government.

During Amin's infamous reign more than a million people were murdered and Christians were often in the frontline of his demonic hatred for human life. In the midst of all this carnage Reinhard's host had survived and at great personal risk had saved countless Christians from being put to death. Idi Amin tolerated a section of the established church, but viciously opposed the Pentecostal/evangelical groups. House meetings were banned. When the feared secret police burst into a house and found people with Bibles or in prayer they were arrested. Amazingly, Reinhard's host had been put in charge of religious affairs and whenever he was told of an impending raid by the secret police he would smuggle a clandestine message to the house groups, who quickly fled.

The three-day crusade had been widely publicised, but Reinhard and his co-workers were puzzled because they could see so few of the hundreds of posters which had been sent on ahead. They expected to see them on most street corners and when they queried this with the organisers they heard something very precious. Because Christian literature is so scarce and because the CFAN posters were so attractive the Christians had pulled them down as fast as they were pasted up and put them up as decorations inside their homes.

Despite the lack of posters the people of Kampala soon knew that Bonnke and team were in town. The venue could not have been better − the city square which was within a stone's throw of the Supreme Court buildings. Right from the first meeting God's power was displayed. Healings were multiplied. Crutches were waved in the air and one woman, tears pouring down her face, testified that her little girl who had been blind, could now see. The crowd burst into joyful praise. It was a wonderful meeting. The rally certainly made an impact, because the meeting the next afternoon was cancelled following complaints from officials at the Supreme Court. The noise from the loudspeakers had interrupted their sittings and they had been forced to close their sessions.

The final meeting on the Sunday afternoon saw about 6 000 people gathered in the square. While preaching, Reinhard noticed ominous black clouds gathering in the sky and huge dust banks swirling towards the city. Not wanting to miss the chance for an altar call he raced through his message, deliberately cutting it short so that he could "pull in the net". Hundreds responded and he had hardly said a final "amen" when giant rain drops started to fall and within seconds the huge crowd were drenched. Reinhard and some pastors took refuge in a parked vehicle and they expected the crowd to disperse. But they just stood, clothing plastered to their skin and water pouring down their faces. Their philosophy was a simple one: we cannot get any wetter than we are. The sight of such a bedraggled crowd touched a cord in Reinhard's heart and he got back onto the platform and began to minister and pray for the sick. Despite all the persecution and hardship, Christianity was very much alive in Uganda. The people were hungry for the gospel and as a servant of God he could not turn his back on these dear people.

When Reinhard passed through the airport terminal on his way home, an immigration officer called him aside and asked: "Are you Pastor Bonnke who preached in the city square? Can you give me a scripture?"

"Yes, replied Reinhard. "Looking unto Jesus, the Author and Finisher of our faith."

As always Reinhard deferred to accept any personal adulation.

As the jet plane clawed itself free of the ground and Reinhard looked down at the city of Kampala he was unconsciously looking for a site for his Big Tent. The

African itinerary for the Big Tent is not going to be easy to draw up once Reinhard turns his face firmly northward into the heart of the continent.

A brief stay at headquarters with a few hurried church meetings, including one to Christian City where Pastor Theo Wolmarans handed over a cheque for R20 000 to CFAN, and then he was off again. This time home to Germany for a month of preaching engagements in September.

Besides seeing some of the biggest crowds in many years, the German preaching tour welded the American connection a bit firmer. Pat Robertson, president of CBN and founder of the famous "700 club" was itching to get a live interview with Reinhard. Because of his almost impossible preaching schedule the interview had to be done via a satellite link-up from Germany.

Arrangements for the interview were all checked out, but the day before the transmission there was a last-minute flurry. Due to an oversight the studio had not been booked. Hurried telephone calls between Germany, South Africa and America managed to salvage the situation. But it was a close call.

Reinhard arrived on time at a studio in Stuttgart where television technicians at the studio were very curious to know why a preacher should warrant VIP treatment with a trans-Atlantic satellite interview. The cost for the 20-minute interview was R20 000 and such link-ups were usually only for politicians.

The interview, by Pat Robertson, went smoothly and the Holy Spirit clearly directed the theme which revolved around the scripture in Joel: "I will pour out My Spirit on all flesh." Viewers in America, waiting for the link-up with Reinhard in Germany, heard Pat

Robertson using this verse and talking about the move of God across the world and when they crossed to Germany Reinhard's opening words contained the same verse, yet he had not known anything of what had been said previously in the transmission. This interview paved the way for a hectic television schedule throughout Canada and America at the end of the year and Reinhard and Robertson would meet face to face over a luncheon that would be of great significance to CFAN.

While in Germany Reinhard sensed a new awakening to spiritual things. He has faithfully returned to his Fatherland year after year and it has often been painful to his soul to see the spiritual famine in his country — and, indeed, throughout western Europe. But this time he was pleasantly surprised and thrilled to see a genuine hunger for the things of God and the number of young people responding to the call to give their lives to Jesus.

While preaching in the Hamburg University auditorium the meeting was interrupted by a man who shouted from the top balcony, "Deceiver, deceiver!" The audience were shocked by the outburst, but not Reinhard because he immediately saw it as a challenge from satan.

"It was the best thing that man could have done because that really switched me on. An anointing of the Holy Spirit swept through that hall and as I preached and challenged the people to make a stand for Jesus young people began to jump up spontaneously. It was a glorious meeting.

"The young people are fed up with all the materialism that has surrounded them in the past. They want reality — and they're finding it in Jesus."

There was an outstanding conversion to Christ during the Hamburg crusade when a hardened criminal came forward to accept Jesus. "I noticed him when he responded to the altar call and the Lord burdened my heart for him. He asked to see me after the meeting and he came back with me to my hotel room.

"What he told me was unbelievable. He was a real gangster. I told him that there was only one way for him — the Zacchaeus way. He had to go to the police and he had to make things right. He asked me to go with him to the police station and so we went that evening.

"Before I left Germany to return home I telephoned this man to see how things were going and he told me that the police were still investigating his case."

Meanwhile, back in Johannesburg the site had been surveyed for the Dedication Day, and Reinhard gave the green light for the two-week crusade in Soweto.

Reinhard hardly had time to unpack his suitcases when, accompanied by general manager, Peter Vandenberg, he jetted out across the Atlantic on an energy-sapping four-week visit to Canada, America and Germany. It proved to be the most fruitful overseas trip of the year.

As the year thundered to a close, the urgency for the trucks to haul the Big Tent became greater. Costs, of course, were the hurdle. It was estimated that R1,5-million was needed for the transport fleet. Without adequate transport it was impossible to move the Big Tent very far from its Witfield headquarters. The Big Tent was much like a whale stranded on the beach at low tide.

Ever since the simple communion service at the Big

Tent at the trial crusade in KwaThema on July 31, Reinhard and the CFAN team had been praying and believing God for 10 trucks by the end of December Money for trucks was promised by several churches and at the "Jesus 83" convention in Durban early in November more money was pledged, but the cash still had to come in. So it was with a real urgency that Reinhard and his general manager left Jan Smuts airport in mid-November. Lined up in Canada and across the US were a series of vital television interviews.

The welcome and the response they received was remarkable. They found that the vision and the mission of the Big Tent was a major talking point among American Christians. The TV programmes were a tremendous success.

Reinhard had lunch with Pat Robertson, of CBN, and Reinhard was able to share personally much of the vision for Africa with this fine man of God. During the luncheon Robertson pledged a substantial amount of money to CFAN for 1984 and in addition another large amount was paid over immediately. Cash for the trucks was, at last, available. But the Lord had an even greater surprise and blessing when Reinhard flew back, stopping off first for a couple of quick meetings in Germany.

Some months earlier Reinhard had heard about a fleet of vehicles which had been ordered by the Libyan government, but which had not been taken up in full.

He went to the vehicle depot which was situated near Hamburg and there, in the yard were row upon row of new, six-wheel drive trucks fitted with hydraulic winches. All the equipment had been specially strengthened for North African conditions.

As he stared at the vehicles he began to feel a surge in his spirit. He was not wrong. The Holy Spirit had led him into one of the best financial deals of his life.

The trucks were for sale − at half price. All that Reinhard needed to do was to respray them. They were all painted in sombre military green. Not only was this an outstanding bargain, but the US dollar was riding high as well and the money he had collected in America was soon spent. He ordered six trucks and ten trailers.

Reinhard couldn't help smiling as he praised God for this provision. "The swords of revolution are being beaten into ploughshares for the gospel. Maybe one day these self same trucks will bring the gospel to Libya."

It was on this triumphant note that Reinhard climaxed 1983.

# CHAPTER 28

# Last word

The work and ministry of Reinhard Bonnke has expanded at an astonishing rate in the past few years. It has brought tremendous blessings, but also pressures and dangers. One of these dangers will haunt Reinhard until he sees Jesus. A danger, though, which he has steered clear of as success and popularity have been heaped into his lap. The danger, of course, is pride.

Christians often place men on pedestals, and then when their human icons get a bit tarnished by the corroding elements of life, they collapse into a heap of despair and disappointment.

When reading of the wonderful and exciting exploits of Reinhard Bonnke one almost automatically places him on a special spiritual level. When a man with his infectious enthusiasm has passed through a village, town or city, he leaves behind bands of adulating supporters. It is these supporters, and they must number hundreds of thousands throughout Africa and the rest of the world, who are the single greatest threat to Reinhard's ministry.

Reinhard is at pains to remain what he honestly believes he is, a "servant of the Lord", and not to allow pride to surface in any area of his life or ministry. To date he has successfully dodged the darts of pride. He has a compassionate heart and that, combined with his openess, his agile, almost gymnastic mind, and his sense of humour, are his defence. This combination, plus of course, his personal devotion to the Lord, should ensure that he never falters. His quick thinking and humour are beautifully illustrated in the following story which took place in the Auckland Park television studios, Johannesburg, before the recording of a religious programme.

Before stepping in front of the cameras Reinhard started a conversation with one of the guest panelists, a well-known actor, whose special qualification for the TV show was the fact that he was a professing atheist. The man was also a keen horse racing fan and it was round about the time of South Africa's most famous turf event the Durban July. Being a man of the world the actor casually asked Reinhard what horse he fancied for the big race!

At this point Reinhard displayed an artful touch to the old fashioned skill of witnessing for Jesus.

"I told him that I was not a gambler, but that the Book of Revelation speaks about a wonderful white horse. The man's ears pricked up at the mention of horse and he asked the question I hoped he would: 'Tell me, who is the jockey?'

"That was what I wanted. 'His Name is Faithful and True, He is the King of Kings and Lord of Lords, His Name is Jesus Christ.' That was one horse and rider that my friend never found on his racecard, but I prayed that the Holy Spirit would bring him into that Heavenly winner's enclosure one day".

Then there was the occasion when a well-meaning optician came to Reinhard with the generous offer of 3 000 free pairs of spectacles. It's said that Reinhard stared at the man for a moment then said: "My friend in our crusades we don't hand out spectacles . . . we collect them!"

It is these touches of humour, embroidered with the serious, that make Reinhard an open, approachable person. He knows he is not perfect and like every other Christian he strives to please his Saviour. He confesses: "I have often pondered why God should bless me with so much. There are far better educated men of God in the world, men just as dedicated . . . why He should choose me . . . I do not know."

Nevertheless, having been chosen Reinhard has accepted the heavenly trust and that is why he boldly and confidently proclaims: "Africa will be saved" — a cry that he believes will echo from Cape Town to Cairo and this story, like the Book of Acts, has no ending because the exploits of the Holy Spirit in the life of Reinhard Bonnke and the Big Tent are only beginning.

# A personal message from Reinhard Bonnke

Dear Readers,
If you have enjoyed this book and would like to know more about the ministry of Christ for all Nations then please write to me at the address given below. I would invite all of you to join with me in believing that Africa will be saved. Your prayers and support are most precious in the eyes of our Lord Jesus Christ.

God bless you,

Reinhard Bonnke
Christ for all Nations
Private Bag
Witfield 1467